Great Jobs
for
Chemistry
Majors

Great Jobs for

Chemistry
Majors

Mark Rowh

Series Developers and Contributing Authors
Stephen E. Lambert
Julie Ann DeGalan

VGM Career Horizons
NTC/Contemporary Publishing Group

02-712

Library of Congress Cataloging-in-Publication Data

Rowh, Mark.
        Great jobs for chemistry majors / Mark Rowh ; series
    developers and contributing authors, Stephen E. Lambert and
    Julie Ann DeGalan.
                p.   cm. — (Great jobs for—)
        Includes index.
        ISBN 0-8442-1915-0
        1. Chemistry—Vocational guidance.   I. Lambert, Stephen E.
    II. DeGalan, Julie.   III. Title.   IV. Series.
    QD39.5.R688   1999
    540'.23'7—dc21   98-46898
                                                                                    CIP

Published by VGM Career Horizons
A division of NTC/Contemporary Publishing Group
4255 West Touhy Avenue, Lincolnwood (Chicago), Illinois 60646-1975 U.S.A.
Copyright © 1999 by NTC/Contemporary Publishing Group, Inc.
Printed in the United States of America
International Standard Book Number: 0-8442-1915-0
99 00 01 02 03 04 MV 18 17 16 15 14 13 12 11 10 9 8 7 6 5 4 3 2 1

To Mr. J. A. McClanahan
and Mr. Elmer Fike

CONTENTS

Acknowledgments

The author offers grateful thanks to the following for their cooperation in providing information for this book:

American Ceramic Society

American Chemical Society

American Institute of Chemical Engineers

American Plastics Council

Arizona State University

Association for the Education of Teachers in Science

Canadian Society for Chemical Engineering

Canadian Society for Chemical Technology

Canadian Society for Chemistry

Chemical Heritage Foundation

Emory and Henry College

The George Washington University

Montana State University

Rutgers University

Salve Regina University

Society of Cosmetic Chemists

Society of Environmental Toxicology and Chemistry

U.S. Department of Labor

U.S. Office of Personnel Management

INTRODUCTION

CHEMISTRY: FORMULA FOR SUCCESS

*I*n your studies to date, you've undoubtedly gained an appreciation for the importance of chemistry in modern life. The understanding of chemistry and the application of that understanding affect everyone. From the development of food preservatives and pesticides to the manufacture of thousands of consumer products ranging from fuel to pain medication, chemistry plays countless roles in improving people's lives.

Naturally, as a chemistry major you already know about the importance of the science of chemistry. But you may not realize that those who study chemistry enjoy a variety of career options.

Perhaps you chose a major in chemistry because you hope to work as a research scientist. That is a common objective, and many students use a bachelor's degree with a major in chemistry as the first step toward attending graduate school and becoming practicing researchers.

On the other hand, maybe you have thought about another career direction, such as teaching. If so, a background in chemistry can prepare you to teach that subject at any of several educational levels. But have you thought about a career in selling chemical products? Or managing a research or industrial operation? Or working as an engineer or a technician? You might be surprised at the variety of jobs held by men and women who have majored in chemistry. In industry, government, business, education, and other areas, those with backgrounds in chemistry can flourish.

THE INSIDE STORY

During college, people are often labeled according to their chosen majors. The art students are seen as "artistic"; the English majors as "humanists"; and you, the chemistry major, as a "techie" or "science whiz." Of course, these labels are simplifications, generalizations, and often just plain wrong. A major cannot and should not define who you are.

Maybe we should stop and consider some terms. Let's start with *chemistry*. If you're a chemistry major or are thinking about majoring in this field, you've probably heard others say, "Oh, I could never be stuck in a lab," or, "I have no head for science," or "That stuff is too technical for me," and other expressions of distaste based on their perceptions of chemistry.

What others may not realize is that all students who major in chemistry do not end up in the same type of job. Some go on to graduate school and become research scientists. Others take jobs in industry immediately following graduation. These jobs may consist of research and development tasks, or may go in an entirely different direction, such as sale of chemical products. Some chemistry majors take jobs with government agencies, dealing with everything from basic research to wastewater treatment. Still others go into teaching, start their own businesses, or end up working for huge corporations.

In short, the world of chemistry is a big one. And it is much more diverse than it might first appear, even to someone who has shown a flair for chemistry and decided to study it intensively.

If you haven't regarded chemistry this way, it's an exciting concept. It means that you can investigate your interests, your personality, and your particular talents and then match them with career activities related to chemistry.

Of course, it's a challenging world out there. That's a message you've encountered from many sources, from your college studies to television news shows. Employment is no longer an absolute given, and even some of the most talented and skilled workers can lose their jobs through mergers, buyouts, and other consolidations as businesses try to enhance profits through economies of size. To remain a contender in this volatile world, you need a clear view not only of chemistry but of yourself as a chemistry major.

The jobs described in the career paths outlined in *Great Jobs for Chemistry Majors* will provide an overview of some promising areas of employment. As you read these chapters, think about which career areas appeal to you. The appeal base will be different for each person. For you, perhaps the most important factors in a job are the skills and knowledge level demanded. Or the primary factor may be the kinds of settings you'd be working in, or the activities you'd be performing. These are all good reasons for pursuing a particular career pathway.

Of the many majors available to a college student, chemistry has long held the promise of being one of the most practical courses of study. It offers real-world applications in the classroom, as well as courses that prepare students for good jobs after graduation. As a chemistry major, you can look to the future with optimism.

THE IDEAL CHEMISTRY GRADUATE

The ideal chemistry graduate might be a specialist. He or she might have concentrated in a specific field of study, such as electrochemistry, preparing to perform a narrow range of duties. Or the ideal chemistry grad might be a generalist, prepared to take on any of a variety of positions. Armed with the analytical and communication skills of the college graduate, plus an understanding of scientific principles, the chemistry grad has much to offer. This is true in the worlds of both work and postgraduate study.

So who is the ideal chemistry graduate? She or he is the person ready to open the doors made possible by the work involved to date. Whether that means going on to advanced studies or entering the workforce, a major in chemistry can open many doors.

Great Jobs

for

Chemistry
Majors

PART ONE

THE JOB SEARCH

CHAPTER ONE

THE SELF-ASSESSMENT

*S*elf-assessment is the process by which you begin to acknowledge your own particular blend of education, experiences, values, needs, and goals. It provides the foundation for career planning and the entire job search process. Self-assessment involves looking inward and asking yourself what can sometimes prove to be difficult questions. This self-examination should lead to an intimate understanding of your personal traits, your personal values, your consumption patterns and economic needs, your longer-term goals, your skill base, your preferred skills, and your under-developed skills.

You come to the self-assessment process knowing yourself well in some of these areas, but you may still be uncertain about other aspects. You may be well aware of your consumption patterns, but have you spent much time specifically identifying your longer-term goals or your personal values as they relate to work? No matter what level of self-assessment you have undertaken to date, it is now time to clarify all of these issues and questions as they relate to the job search.

The knowledge you gain in the self-assessment process will guide the rest of your job search. In this book, you will learn about all of the following tasks:

- Writing resumes
- Exploring possible job titles
- Identifying employment sites
- Networking
- Interviewing
- Following up
- Evaluating job offers

In each of these steps, you will rely on and return often to the understanding gained through your self-assessment. Any individual seeking employment must be able and willing to express these facets of his or her personality to recruiters and interviewers throughout the job search. This communication allows you to show the world who you are so that together with employers you can determine whether there will be a workable match with a given job or career path.

HOW TO CONDUCT A SELF-ASSESSMENT

The self-assessment process goes on naturally all the time. People ask you to clarify what you mean, or you make a purchasing decision, or you begin a new relationship. You react to the world and the world reacts to you. How you understand these interactions and any changes you might make because of them are part of the natural process of self-discovery. There is, however, a more comprehensive and efficient way to approach self-assessment with regard to employment.

Because self-assessment can become a complex exercise, we have distilled it into a seven-step process that provides an effective basis for undertaking a job search. The seven steps include the following:

1. Understanding your personal traits

2. Identifying your personal values

3. Calculating your economic needs

4. Exploring your longer-term goals

5. Enumerating your skill base

6. Recognizing your preferred skills

7. Assessing skills needing further development

As you work through your self-assessment, you might want to create a worksheet similar to the one shown in Exhibit 1.1. Or you might want to keep a journal of the thoughts you have as you undergo this process. There will be many opportunities to revise your self-assessment as you start down the path of seeking a career.

STEP 1 Understanding Your Personal Traits

Each person has a unique personality that he or she brings to the job search process. Gaining a better understanding of your personal traits can help you

---

Exhibit 1.1

Self-Assessment Worksheet

STEP 1. Understand Your Personal Traits
The personal traits that describe me are:
(Include all of the words that describe you.)

The ten personal traits that most accurately describe me are: *(List these ten traits.)*

STEP 2. Identify Your Personal Values
Working conditions that are important to me include:
(List working conditions that would have to exist for you to accept a position.)

The values that go along with my working conditions are:
(Write down the values that correspond to each working condition.)

Some additional values I've decided to include are:
(List those values you identify as you conduct this job search.)

STEP 3. Calculate Your Economic Needs
My estimated minimum annual salary requirement is:
(Write the salary you have calculated based on your budget.)

Starting salaries for the positions I'm considering are:
(List the name of each job you are considering and the associated starting salary.)

STEP 4. Explore Your Longer-Term Goals
My thoughts on longer-term goals right now are:
(Jot down some of your longer-term goals as you know them right now.)

STEP 5. Enumerate Your Skill Base

The general skills I possess are:
(List the skills that underlie tasks you are able to complete.)

The specific skills I possess are:
(List more technical or specific skills that you possess and indicate your level of expertise.)

General and specific skills that I want to promote to employers for the jobs I'm considering are:
(List general and specific skills for each type of job you are considering.)

STEP 6. Recognize Your Preferred Skills

Skills that I would like to use on the job include:
(List skills that you hope to use on the job, and indicate how often you'd like to use them.)

STEP 7. Assess Skills Needing Further Development

Some skills that I'll need to acquire for the jobs I'm considering include:
(Write down skills listed in job advertisements or job descriptions that you don't currently possess.)

I believe I can build these skills by:
(Describe how you plan to acquire these skills.)

evaluate job and career choices. Identifying these traits, then finding employment that allows you to draw on at least some of them can create a rewarding and fulfilling work experience. If potential employment doesn't allow you to use these preferred traits, it is important to decide whether you can find other ways to express them or whether you would be better off not considering this type of job. Interests and hobbies pursued outside of work hours can be one way to use personal traits you don't have an opportunity to draw on in your work. For example, if you consider yourself an outgoing person and the kinds of jobs you are examining allow little contact with other people, you may be able to achieve the level of interaction that is comfortable for you outside of your work setting. If such a compromise seems impractical or otherwise unsatisfactory, you probably should explore only jobs that provide the interaction you want and need on the job.

Many young adults who are not very confident about their attractiveness to employers will downplay their need for income. They will say, "Money is not all that important if I love my work." But if you begin to document exactly what you need for housing, transportation, insurance, clothing, food, and utilities, you will begin to understand that some jobs cannot meet your financial needs and it doesn't matter how wonderful the job is. If you have to worry each payday about bills and other financial obligations, you won't be very effective on the job. Begin now to be honest with yourself about your needs.

Inventorying Your Personal Traits. Begin the self-assessment process by creating an inventory of your personal traits. Using the list in Exhibit 1.2, decide which of these personal traits describe you.

Exhibit 1.2

Accurate	Courageous	Friendly
Active	Critical	Future-oriented
Adaptable	Curious	Generous
Adventurous	Daring	Gentle
Affectionate	Decisive	Good-natured
Aggressive	Deliberate	Helpful
Ambitious	Detail-oriented	Honest
Analytical	Determined	Humorous
Appreciative	Discreet	Idealistic
Artistic	Dominant	Imaginative
Brave	Eager	Impersonal
Businesslike	Easygoing	Independent
Calm	Efficient	Individualistic
Capable	Emotional	Industrious
Caring	Empathetic	Informal
Cautious	Energetic	Innovative
Cheerful	Excitable	Intellectual
Clean	Expressive	Intelligent
Competent	Extroverted	Introverted
Confident	Fair-minded	Intuitive
Conscientious	Farsighted	Inventive
Conservative	Feeling	Jovial
Considerate	Firm	Just
Cool	Flexible	Kind
Cooperative	Formal	Liberal

Likable	Practical	Serious
Logical	Precise	Sincere
Loyal	Principled	Sociable
Mature	Private	Spontaneous
Methodical	Productive	Strong
Meticulous	Progressive	Strong-minded
Mistrustful	Quick	Structured
Modest	Quiet	Subjective
Motivated	Rational	Tactful
Objective	Realistic	Thorough
Observant	Receptive	Thoughtful
Open-minded	Reflective	Tolerant
Opportunistic	Relaxed	Trusting
Optimistic	Reliable	Trustworthy
Organized	Reserved	Truthful
Original	Resourceful	Understanding
Outgoing	Responsible	Unexcitable
Patient	Reverent	Uninhibited
Peaceable	Sedentary	Verbal
Personable	Self-confident	Versatile
Persuasive	Self-controlled	Wholesome
Pleasant	Self-disciplined	Wise
Poised	Sensible	
Polite	Sensitive	

Focusing on Selected Personal Traits. Of all the traits you identified from the list in Exhibit 1.2, select the ten you believe most accurately describe you. If you are having a difficult time deciding, think about which words people who know you well would use to describe you. Keep track of these ten traits.

Considering Your Personal Traits in the Job Search Process. As you begin exploring jobs and careers, watch for matches between your personal traits and the job descriptions you read. Some jobs will require many personal traits you know you possess, and others will not seem to match those traits.

• •

Working as a laboratory supervisor, for example, will draw upon your organizational, analytical, and communicative skills. You will need to gather and analyze information,

keep track of work conducted, assign tasks to lab personnel, and perform a variety of supervisory functions.
This might range from ordering supplies to writing a
grant proposal or completing performance evaluations.
You might work with different levels of staff, including
lab technicians, chemists, and clerical staff. With a variety of tasks to be accomplished, the job will demand attention to detail and a good memory.

· ·

Your ability to respond to changing conditions, decision-making ability,
productivity, creativity, and verbal skills all have a bearing on your success
in and enjoyment of your work life. To better guarantee success, be sure to
take the time needed to understand these traits in yourself.

STEP 2 Identifying Your Personal Values

Your personal values affect every aspect of your life, including employment,
and they develop and change as you move through life. Values can be defined
as principles that we hold in high regard, qualities that are important and
desirable to us. Some values aren't ordinarily connected to work (love, beauty,
color, light, marriage, family, or religion), and others are (autonomy, cooperation, effectiveness, achievement, knowledge, and security). Our values
determine, in part, the level of satisfaction we feel in a particular job.

Defining Acceptable Working Conditions. One facet of employment is the set
of working conditions that must exist for someone to consider taking a job.
    Each of us would probably create a unique list of acceptable working con-
ditions, but items that might be included on many people's lists are the
amount of money you would need to be paid, how far you are willing to
drive or travel, the amount of freedom you want in determining your own
schedule, whether you would be working with people or data or things, and
the types of tasks you would be willing to do. Your conditions might include
statements of working conditions you will *not* accept; for example, you might
not be willing to work at night or on weekends or holidays.
    If you were offered a job tomorrow, what conditions would have to exist
for you to realistically consider accepting the position? Take some time and
make a list of these conditions.

Realizing Associated Values. Your list of working conditions can be used to
create an inventory of your values relating to jobs and careers you are exploring. For example, if one of your conditions stated that you wanted to earn

---

Exhibit 1.3

Work Values

Achievement	Development	Physical activity
Advancement	Effectiveness	Power
Adventure	Excitement	Precision
Attainment	Fast pace	Prestige
Authority	Financial gain	Privacy
Autonomy	Helping	Profit
Belonging	Humor	Recognition
Challenge	Improvisation	Risk
Change	Independence	Security
Communication	Influencing others	Self-expression
Community	Intellectual stimulation	Solitude
Competition	Interaction	Stability
Completion	Knowledge	Status
Contribution	Leading	Structure
Control	Mastery	Supervision
Cooperation	Mobility	Surroundings
Creativity	Moral fulfillment	Time freedom
Decision making	Organization	Variety

---

at least $25,000 per year, the associated value would be financial gain. If another condition was that you wanted to work with a friendly group of people, the value that goes along with that might be belonging or interaction with people. Exhibit 1.3 provides a list of commonly held values that relate to the work environment; use it to create your own list of personal values.

Relating Your Values to the World of Work. As you read the job descriptions in this book and in other suggested resources, think about the values associated with each position.

> For example, in working as a research chemist, your duties may include writing laboratory reports or grant proposals, sending E-mail messages to fellow researchers, and talking on the telephone with colleagues or representatives of funding agencies.

If you were thinking about a career in this field, or any other field you're exploring, at least some of the associated values should match those you extracted from your list of working conditions. Take a second look at any values that don't match up. How important are they to you? What will happen if they are not satisfied on the job? Can you incorporate those personal values elsewhere? Your answers need to be brutally honest. As you continue your exploration, be sure to add to your list any additional values that occur to you.

STEP 3   Calculating Your Economic Needs

Each of us grew up in an environment that provided for certain basic needs, such as food and shelter, and, to varying degrees, other needs that we now consider basic, such as cable TV, reading materials, or an automobile. Needs such as privacy, space, and quiet, which at first glance may not appear to be monetary needs, may add to housing expenses and so should be considered as you examine your economic needs. For example, if you place a high value on a large, open living space for yourself, it would be difficult to satisfy that need without an associated high housing cost, especially in a densely populated city environment.

As you prepare to move into the world of work and become responsible for meeting your own basic needs, it is important to consider the salary you will need to be able to afford a satisfying standard of living. The three-step process outlined here will help you plan a budget, which in turn will allow you to evaluate the various career choices and geographic locations you are considering. The steps include (1) developing a realistic budget, (2) examining starting salaries, and (3) using a cost-of-living index.

Developing a Realistic Budget. Each of us has certain expectations for the kind of lifestyle we want to maintain. In order to begin the process of defining your economic needs, it will be helpful to determine what you expect to spend on routine monthly expenses. These expenses include housing, food, transportation, entertainment, utilities, loan repayments, and revolving charge accounts. A worksheet that details many of these expenses is shown in Exhibit 1.4. You may not currently spend for certain items, but you probably

---

Exhibit 1.4

Estimated Monthly Expenses Worksheet

		Could Reduce Spending? (Yes/No)
Cable	$ _____	_____
Child care	_____	_____

		Could Reduce Spending? (Yes/No)
Clothing	_____	_____
Educational loan repayment	_____	_____
Entertainment	_____	_____
Food	_____	_____
At home	_____	_____
Meals out	_____	_____
Gifts	_____	_____
Housing		
Rent/mortgage	_____	_____
Insurance	_____	_____
Property taxes	_____	_____
Medical insurance	_____	_____
Reading materials		
Newspapers	_____	_____
Magazines	_____	_____
Books	_____	_____
Revolving loans/charges	_____	_____
Savings	_____	_____
Telephone	_____	_____
Transportation		
Auto payment	_____	_____
Insurance	_____	_____
Parking	_____	_____
Gasoline	_____	_____
or		
Cab/train/bus fare	_____	_____
Utilities		
Electric	_____	_____
Gas	_____	_____
Water/sewer	_____	_____
Vacations	_____	_____
Miscellaneous expense 1	_____	_____
Expense: _____		
Miscellaneous expense 2	_____	_____
Expense: _____		
Miscellaneous expense 3	_____	_____
Expense: _____		

TOTAL MONTHLY EXPENSES:_____

YEARLY EXPENSES (Monthly expenses $\times$ 12): _____

INCREASE TO INCLUDE TAXES (Yearly expenses $\times$ 1.35): _____ =

MINIMUM ANNUAL SALARY REQUIREMENT _____

will have to once you begin supporting yourself. As you develop this budget, be generous in your estimates, but keep in mind any items that could be reduced or eliminated. If you are not sure about the cost of a certain item, talk with family or friends who would be able to give you a realistic estimate.

If this is new or difficult for you, start to keep a log of expenses right now. You may be surprised at how much you actually spend each month for food or stamps or magazines. Household expenses and personal grooming items can often loom very large in a budget, as can auto repairs or home maintenance.

Income taxes must also be taken into consideration when examining salary requirements. State and local taxes vary by location, so it is difficult to calculate exactly the effect of taxes on the amount of income you need to generate. To roughly estimate the gross income necessary to generate your minimum annual salary requirement, multiply the minimum salary you have calculated (see Exhibit 1.4) by a factor of 1.35. The resulting figure will be an approximation of what your gross income would need to be, given your estimated expenses.

Examining Starting Salaries. Starting salaries for each of the career tracks are provided throughout this book. These salary figures can be used in conjunction with the cost-of-living index (discussed in the next section) to determine whether you would be able to meet your basic economic needs in a given geographic location.

Using a Cost-of-Living Index. If you are thinking about trying to get a job in a geographic region other than the one where you now live, understanding differences in the cost of living will help you come to a more informed decision about making a move. By using a cost-of-living index, you can compare salaries offered and the cost of living in different locations with what you know about the salaries offered and the cost of living in your present location.

Many variables are used to calculate the cost-of-living index, including housing expenses, groceries, utilities, transportation, health care, clothing, entertainment, local income taxes, and local sales taxes. Cost-of-living indices can be found in many resources, such as *Equal Employment Opportunity Bimonthly, Places Rated Almanac,* or *The Best Towns in America.* They are constantly being recalculated based on changes in costs.

. . . .

If you lived in Cleveland, Ohio, for example, and you were interested in working as a sales representative for a chemical manufacturing firm, you would earn, on average, $25,784 annually. But let's say you're thinking about moving to either New York, Los Angeles, or Denver. You know you can live on $25,784 in Cleveland, but you want to be able to equal that salary in other locations you're considering. How much will you need to earn in those locations to do this? Figuring the cost of living for each city will show you.

Let's walk through this example. In any cost-of-living index, the number 100 represents the national average cost of living, and each city is assigned an index number based on current prices in that city for the items included in the index (housing, food, etc.). In the index we used, New York was assigned the number 213.3, Los Angeles' index was 124.6, Denver's was 100.0, and Cleveland's index was 114.3. In other words, it costs more than twice as much to live in New York as it does in Denver. We can set up a table to determine exactly how much you would have to earn in each of these cities to have the same buying power that you have in Cleveland.

Job: Sales representative for a chemical manufacturing firm

CITY	INDEX	EQUIVALENT SALARY
New York / Cleveland	$\frac{213.3}{114.3}$	$\times$ \$25,784 = \$48,116 in New York
Los Angeles / Cleveland	$\frac{124.6}{114.3}$	$\times$ \$25,784 = \$28,107 in Los Angeles
Denver / Cleveland	$\frac{100.0}{114.3}$	$\times$ \$25,784 = \$22,558 in Denver

---

You would have to earn $48,116 in New York, $28,107 in Los Angeles, and $22,558 in Denver to match the buying power of $25,784 in Cleveland.

If you would like to determine whether it's financially worthwhile to make any of these moves, one more piece of information is needed: the salaries of sales representatives in these other cities. The *American Salaries and Wages*

Survey reports such information. Here is a sample of salaries for sales representatives.

	Annual Salary	Salary Equivalent to Ohio	Change in Buying Power
New York	$48,115	$70,605	−$22,490
Los Angeles	$43,114	$41,244	+$ 1,870
Denver	$35,364	$33,101	+$ 2,263
Cleveland	$37,835	—	—

If you moved to New York City and secured employment as a sales representative, you would not be able to maintain a lifestyle similar to the one you led in Cleveland; in fact, you would have to add almost 50 percent to your income to maintain a similar lifestyle in New York. The same would not be true for a move to Los Angeles or Denver. You would increase your buying power given the rate of pay and cost of living in these cities.

....

You can work through a similar exercise for any type of job you are considering and for many locations when current salary information is available. It will be worth your time to undertake this analysis if you are seriously considering a relocation. By doing so you will be able to make an informed choice.

STEP 4 Exploring Your Longer-Term Goals

There is no question that when we first begin working, our goals are to use our skills and education in a job that will reward us with employment, income, and status relative to the preparation we brought with us to this position. If we are not being paid as much as we feel we should for our level of education, or if job demands don't provide the intellectual stimulation we had hoped for, we experience unhappiness and as a result often seek other employment.

Most jobs we consider "good" are those that fulfill our basic "lower-level" needs of security, food, clothing, shelter, income, and productive work. But even when our basic needs are met and our jobs are secure and productive, we as individuals are constantly changing. As we change, the demands and expectations we place on our jobs may change. Fortunately, some jobs grow and change with us, and this explains why some people are happy through-out many years in a job.

But more often people are bigger than the jobs they fill. We have more goals and needs than any job could fulfill. These are "higher-level" needs of self-esteem, companionship, affection, and an increasing desire to feel we are employing ourselves in the most effective way possible. Not all of these higher-level needs can be fulfilled through employment, but for as long as we are employed, we increasingly demand that our jobs play their part in moving us along the path to fulfillment.

Another obvious but important fact is that we change as we mature. Although our jobs also have the potential for change, they may not change as frequently or as markedly as we do. There are increasingly fewer one-job, one-employer careers; we must think about a work future that may involve voluntary or forced moves from employer to employer. Because of that very real possibility, we need to take advantage of the opportunities in each position we hold to acquire skills and competencies that will keep us viable and attractive as employees in a job market that is not only increasingly technology/computer dependent, but also is populated with more and more small, self-transforming organizations rather than the large, seemingly stable organizations of the past.

It may be difficult in the early stages of the job search to determine whether the path you are considering can meet these longer-term goals. Reading about career paths and individual career histories in your field can be very helpful in this regard. Meeting and talking with individuals further along in their careers can be enlightening as well. Older workers can provide valuable guidance on "self-managing" your career, which will become an increasingly valuable skill in the future. Some of these ideas may seem remote as you read this now, but you should be able to appreciate the need to ensure that you are growing, developing valuable new skills, and researching other employers who might be interested in your particular skills package.

· ·

If you are considering a position as a research chemist, you would gain a better perspective on this career by talking to an entry-level researcher or assistant; a more senior and experienced research chemist; and finally, a manager in an industrial or nonprofit laboratory who has had a considerable work history in chemical research. Each will have a different perspective, unique concerns, and an individual set of value priorities.

· ·

STEP 5   Enumerating Your Skill Base

In terms of the job search, skills can be thought of as capabilities that can be developed in school, at work, or by volunteering and then used in specific job settings. Many studies have documented the kinds of skills that employers seek in entry-level applicants. For example, some of the most desired skills for individuals interested in the teaching profession include the ability to interact effectively with students one on one, to manage a classroom, to adapt to varying situations as necessary, and to get involved in school activities. Business employers have also identified important qualities, including enthusiasm for the employer's product or service, a businesslike mind, the ability to follow written or verbal instructions, the ability to demonstrate self-control, the confidence to suggest new ideas, the ability to communicate with all members of a group, awareness of cultural differences, and loyalty, to name just a few. You will find that many of these skills are also in the repertoire of qualities demanded in your college major.

In order to be successful in obtaining any given job, you must be able to demonstrate that you possess a certain mix of skills that will allow you to carry out the duties required by that job. This skill mix will vary a great deal from job to job; to determine the skills necessary for the jobs you are seeking, you can read job advertisements or more generic job descriptions, such as those found later in this book. If you want to be effective in the job search, you must directly show employers that you possess the skills needed to be successful in filling the position. These skills will initially be described on your resume and then discussed again during the interview process.

Skills are either general or specific. General skills are those that are developed throughout the college years by taking classes, being employed, and getting involved in other related activities such as volunteer work or campus organizations. General skills include the ability to read and write, to perform computations, to think critically, and to communicate effectively. Specific skills are also acquired on the job and in the classroom, but they allow you to complete tasks that require specialized knowledge. Computer programming, drafting, language translating, and copyediting are just a few examples of specific skills that may relate to a given job.

In order to develop a list of skills relevant to employers, you must first identify the general skills you possess, then list specific skills you have to offer, and, finally, examine which of these skills employers are seeking.

Identifying Your General Skills. Because you possess or will possess a college degree, employers will assume that you can read and write, perform certain basic computations, think critically, and communicate effectively. Employers will want to see that you have acquired these skills, and they will want to know which additional general skills you possess.

One way to begin identifying skills is to write an experiential diary. An experiential diary lists all the tasks you were responsible for completing for each job you've held and then outlines the skills required to do those tasks. You may list several skills for any given task. This diary allows you to distinguish between the tasks you performed and the underlying skills required to complete those tasks. Here's an example:

Tasks	Skills
Answering telephone	Effective use of language, clear diction, ability to direct inquiries, ability to solve problems
Waiting on tables	Poise under conditions of time and pressure, speed, accuracy, good memory, simultaneous completion of tasks, sales skills

For each job or experience you have participated in, develop a worksheet based on the example shown here. On a resume, you may want to describe these skills rather than simply listing tasks. Skills are easier for the employer to appreciate, especially when your experience is very different from the employment you are seeking. In addition to helping you identify general skills, this experiential diary will prepare you to speak more effectively in an interview about the qualifications you possess.

Identifying Your Specific Skills. It may be easier to identify your specific skills because you can definitely say whether you can speak other languages, program a computer, draft a map or diagram, or edit a document using appropriate symbols and terminology.

Using your experiential diary, identify the points in your history where you learned how to do something very specific, and decide whether you have a beginning, intermediate, or advanced knowledge of how to use that particular skill. Right now, be sure to list *every* specific skill you have, and don't consider whether you like using the skill. Write down a list of specific skills you have acquired and the level of competence you possess—beginning, intermediate, or advanced.

Relating Your Skills to Employers. You probably have thought about a couple of different jobs you might be interested in obtaining, and one way to begin relating the general and specific skills you possess to a potential employer's needs is to read actual advertisements for these types of positions (see Part Two for resources listing actual job openings).

. . . .

For example, you might be interested in working as a research chemist for a government agency that deals with natural resources, prior to returning to graduate school to seek a doctorate in chemistry with a specialty in organic chemistry. A typical job listing might read, "Conduct laboratory experiments in the chemistry of wood products and related materials. Bachelor's degree in chemistry or science major with at least thirty semester hours in chemistry required. Laboratory work experience preferred." You could then use any one of a number of sources of information that describes the job of research chemist. Chemists in this area conduct laboratory experiments, complete written reports, study developments in the field, replicate experiments performed by others, and develop plans for new experiments. Junior personnel also complete a variety of tasks assigned by senior researchers.

Begin building a comprehensive list of required skills with the first job descriptions you read. Exploring advertisements for several types of related positions will reveal an important core of skills necessary for obtaining the type of work you're interested in. Include both general and specific skills.

Following is a sample list of skills needed to be successful as a research chemist.

Job: Research chemist	
General Skills	**Specific Skills**
Calculating	Determine chemical quantities
Reading	Track development of research related to work
Gathering information	Compile research data
Decision making	Evaluate alternatives
Meeting deadlines	Prepare reports
Attending meetings	Communicating recommendations for research methodology
Entering data into computer	Prepare daily research notes
Writing	Edit reports

On separate sheets of paper, try to generate a list of required skills for at least one job you are considering.

The list of general skills that you develop for a given career path would be valuable for any number of jobs you might seek. Many specific skills would also be transferable to other types of positions. For example, editing reports is a required skill for other types of chemists and other scientists, and for almost any management position. The ability to use basic word processing and spreadsheet software would also be useful in almost any job setting.

....

Now review the list of skills you developed and check off those skills that *you know you possess* and that are required for jobs you are considering. You should refer to these specific skills on the resume that you write for this type of job. See Chapter 2 for details on resume writing.

STEP 6 Recognizing Your Preferred Skills

In the previous section you developed a comprehensive list of skills that relate to particular career paths that are of interest to you. You can now relate these to skills that you prefer to use. We all use a wide range of skills (some researchers say individuals have a repertoire of about 500 skills), but we may not be particularly interested in using all of them in our work. There may be some skills that come to us more naturally or that we use successfully time and time again and that we want to continue to use; these are best described as our preferred skills. For this exercise use the list of skills that you developed for the previous section and decide which of them you are *most interested in using* in future work and how often you would like to use them. You might be interested in using some skills only occasionally, while others you would like to use more regularly. You probably also have skills that you hope you can use constantly.

As you examine job announcements, look for matches between this list of preferred skills and the qualifications described in the advertisements. These skills should be highlighted on your resume and discussed in job interviews.

STEP 7 Assessing Skills Needing Further Development

Previously you developed a list of general and specific skills required for given positions. You already possess some of these skills; those that remain to be developed are your underdeveloped skills.

If you are just beginning the job search, there may be gaps between the qualifications required for some of the jobs being considered and skills you possess. These are your underdeveloped skills. The thought of having to admit to and talk about these underdeveloped skills, especially in a job interview, is a frightening one. One way to put a healthy perspective on this subject is to target and relate your exploration of underdeveloped skills to the types of positions you are seeking. Recognizing these shortcomings and planning to overcome them with either on-the-job training or additional formal education can be a positive way to address the concept of underdeveloped skills.

On your worksheet or in your journal, make a list of up to five general or specific skills required for the positions you're interested in that you *don't currently possess.* For each item list an idea you have for specific action you could take to acquire that skill. Do some brainstorming to come up with possible actions. If you have a hard time generating ideas, talk to people currently working in this type of position, professionals in your college career services office, trusted friends, family members, or members of related professional associations.

If, for example, you are interested in a job for which you don't have some specific required experience, you could locate training opportunities such as classes or workshops offered through a local college or university, community college, or club or association that would help you build the level of expertise you need for the job.

Many excellent jobs in today's economy demand computer skills you probably already have. Most graduates are not so lucky and have to acquire these skills—often before an employer will give their application serious consideration. So, what can you do if you find there are certain skills you're missing? If you're still in school, try to fill the gaps in your knowledge before you graduate. If you've already graduated, look at evening programs, continuing education courses, or tutorial programs that may be available commercially. Developing a modest level of expertise will encourage you to be more confident in suggesting to potential employers that you can continue to add to your skill base on the job.

In Chapter 5 on interviewing we will discuss in detail how to effectively address questions about underdeveloped skills. Generally speaking, though, employers want genuine answers to these types of questions. They want you to reveal "the real you," and they also want to see how you answer difficult questions. In taking the positive, targeted approach discussed above, you show the employer that you are willing to continue to learn and that you have a plan for strengthening your job qualifications.

USING YOUR SELF-ASSESSMENT

Exploring entry-level career options can be an exciting experience if you have good resources available and will take the time to use them. Can you effectively complete the following tasks?

1. Understand and relate your personality traits to career choices.

2. Define your personal values.

3. Determine your economic needs.

4. Explore longer-term goals.

5. Understand your skill base.

6. Recognize your preferred skills.

7. Express a willingness to improve on your underdeveloped skills.

If so, then you can more meaningfully participate in the job search process by writing a more effective resume, finding job titles that represent work you are interested in doing, locating job sites that will provide the opportunity for you to use your strengths and skills, networking in an informed way, participating in focused interviews, getting the most out of follow-up contacts, and evaluating job offers to find those that create a good match between you and the employer.

The remaining chapters guide you through these next steps in the job search process. For many job seekers, this process can take anywhere from three months to a year to implement. The time you will need to put into your job search will depend on the type of job you want and the geographic location where you'd like to work. Think of your effort as a job in itself, requiring you to set aside time each week to complete the needed work. Carefully undertaken efforts may reduce the time you need for your job search.

CHAPTER TWO

THE RESUME AND COVER LETTER

The task of writing a resume may seem overwhelming if you are unfamiliar with this type of document, but there are some easily understood techniques that can and should be used. This section was written to help you understand the purpose of the resume, the different types of resume formats available, and how to write the sections of information traditionally found on a resume. We will present examples and explanations that address questions frequently posed by people writing their first resume or updating an old resume.

Even within the formats and suggestions given below, however, there are infinite variations. True, most resumes follow one of the outlines suggested below, but you should feel free to adjust the resume to suit your needs and make it expressive of your life and experience.

WHY WRITE A RESUME?

The purpose of a resume is to convince an employer that you should be interviewed. You'll want to present enough information to show that you can make an immediate and valuable contribution to an organization. A resume is not an in-depth historical or legal document; later in the job search process you'll be asked to document your entire work history on an application form and attest to its validity. The resume should, instead, highlight relevant information pertaining directly to the organization that will receive the document or the type of position you are seeking.

We will discuss four types of resumes in this chapter: chronological resume, functional resume, targeted resume, and the broadcast letter. The reasons for using one type of resume over another and the typical format for each are addressed in the following sections.

THE CHRONOLOGICAL RESUME

The chronological resume is the most common of the various resume formats and therefore the format that employers are most used to receiving. This type of resume is easy to read and understand because it details the chronological progression of jobs you have held. (See Exhibit 2.1.) It begins with your most recent employment and works back in time. If you have a solid work history or have experience that provided growth and development in your duties and responsibilities, a chronological resume will highlight these achievements. The typical elements of a chronological resume include the heading, a career objective, educational background, employment experience, activities, and references.

The Heading

The heading consists of your name, address, and telephone number. Recently it has come to include fax numbers and electronic mail addresses as well. We suggest that you spell out your full name and type it in all capital letters in bold type. After all, you are the focus of the resume! If you have a current as well as a permanent address and you include both in the heading, be sure to indicate until what date your current address will be valid. Don't forget to include the zip code with your address and the area code with your telephone number.

The Objective

As you formulate the wording for this part of your resume, keep the following points in mind.

The Objective Focuses the Resume. Without a doubt this is the most challenging part of the resume for most resume writers. Even for individuals who have quite firmly decided on a career path, it can be difficult to encapsulate all they want to say in one or two brief sentences. For job seekers who are unfocused or unclear about their intentions, trying to write this section can inhibit the entire resume writing process.

Recruiters tell us, time and again, that the objective creates a frame of reference for them. It helps them see how you express your goals and career

Exhibit 2.1

Chronological Resume

LISA ANNE EMORY

Apartment G-14
Oak Park Extension
Athens, GA 30064
(770) 555-6636

OBJECTIVE
Position teaching chemistry in a high school setting

EDUCATION
Bachelor of Science, Clemson University
Clemson, South Carolina, May 1999
Major: Chemistry
Minor: Teacher Education

Honors/Activities: President, Chemistry Club
Member, Beta Iota Tau (science honorary
society)
Dean's List two semesters, President's List
four semesters
Co-recipient, Rudolf C. Hingis Award as
outstanding undergraduate in chemistry
Magna cum laude graduate

EXPERIENCE
Tutor, Clemson University Success Center, 1997–98
Provided tutoring assistance in chemistry, math, and physics
for non-science majors.
Summer Intern, Myers Chemical Corporation, Spartanburg, South
Carolina, 1998
Conducted laboratory and field research in development of
polymer processes
Kennel Worker, Unity Animal Hospital, Athens, Georgia, 1995–97
(part time and summers)

Provided basic functions in maintaining kennel operations

COMMUNITY SERVICE
Active volunteer with church activities; election-day poll worker;
Habitat for Humanity volunteer

REFERENCES
A selection of both personal and professional references will be
provided on request.

focus. In addition, the statement may indicate in what ways you can immediately benefit an organization. Given the importance of the objective, every
point covered in the resume should relate to it. If information doesn't relate,
it should be omitted. With the word processing technology available today,
each resume can and should be tailored for individual employers or specific
positions that are available.

Choose an Appropriate Length. Because of the brevity necessary for a resume,
you should keep the objective as short as possible. Although objectives of only
four or five words often don't show much direction, objectives that take three
full lines would be viewed as too wordy and might possibly be ignored.

Consider Which Type of Objective Statement You Will Use. There are many ways
to state an objective, but generally there are four forms this statement can
take: (1) a very general statement; (2) a statement focused on a specific position; (3) a statement focused on a specific industry; or (4) a summary of your
qualifications. In our contacts with employers, we often hear that many
resumes don't exhibit any direction or career goals, so we suggest avoiding
general statements when possible.

1. General Objective Statement. General objective statements look like the
following:

- ❑ An entry-level educational programming coordinator position
- ❑ An entry-level marketing position

This type of objective would be useful if you know what type of job you
want but you're not sure which industries interest you.

2. *Position-Focused Objective.* Following are examples of objectives focusing on a specific position:

- ❏ To obtain the position of director of research at the State Council for Environmental Quality

- ❏ To obtain a position as assistant director of research

When a student applies for an advertised job opening, this type of focus can be very effective. The employer knows that the applicant has taken the time to tailor the resume specifically for this position.

3. *Industry-Focused Objective.* Focusing on a particular industry in an objective could be stated as follows:

- ❏ To begin a career as a sales representative in the chemical production industry

4. *Summary of Qualifications Statement.* The summary of qualifications can be used instead of an objective or in conjunction with an objective. The purpose of this type of statement is to highlight relevant qualifications gained through a variety of experiences. This type of statement is often used by individuals with extensive and diversified work experience. An example of a qualifications statement follows:

· ·

A degree in chemistry and three years of progressively increasing job responsibility in an industrial setting have prepared me to begin a career as a researcher in a corporate or nonprofit research agency where thoroughness and attention to detail are valued.

· ·

Support Your Objective. A resume that contains any one of these types of objective statements should then go on to demonstrate why you are qualified to get the position. Listing academic degrees can be one way to indicate qualifications. Another demonstration would be in the way previous experiences, both volunteer and paid, are described. Without this kind of documentation in the body of the resume, the objective looks unsupported. Think of the resume as telling a connected story about you. All the elements should work together to form a coherent picture that ideally should relate to your statement of objective.

Education

This section of your resume should indicate the exact name of the degree you will receive or have received, spelled out completely with no abbreviations. The degree is generally listed after the objective, followed by the institution name and address, and then the month and year of graduation. This section could also include your academic minor, grade point average (GPA), and appearance on the Dean's List or President's List.

If you have enough space, you might want to include a section listing courses related to the field in which you are seeking work. The best use of a "related courses" section would be to list some course work that is not traditionally associated with the major. Perhaps you took several computer courses outside your degree that will be helpful and related to the job prospects you are entertaining. Several education section examples are shown here:

••

- Bachelor of Science Degree in Chemistry
  Ohio State University, Columbus, Ohio, May 1999
  Minor: Physics

- Bachelor of Science Degree with Major in
     Chemistry
  Emory and Henry College, Emory, Virginia,
     May 1999
  Minors: Biology, Computer Science

- Bachelor of Science Degree in Chemical Engineering
  Iowa State University, Ames, Iowa, May 1998
  General Chemistry option
  Minor in Mathematics

An example of a format for a related course section follows:

RELATED COURSES	
General Chemistry	Analytical Chemistry
Physical Chemistry	Inorganic Chemistry
General Organic Chemistry	Organic Chemistry for Majors
Biophysical Chemistry	Instrumental Analysis

••

Experience

The experience section of your resume should be the most substantial part and should take up most of the space on the page. Employers want to see what kind of work history you have. They will look at your range of experiences, longevity in jobs, and specific tasks you are able to complete. This section may also be called "work experience," "related experience," "employment history," or "employment." No matter what you call this section, some important points to remember are the following:

1. **Describe your duties** as they relate to the position you are seeking.

2. **Emphasize major responsibilities** and indicate increases in responsibility. Include all relevant employment experiences: summer, part-time, internships, cooperative education, or self-employment.

3. **Emphasize skills,** especially those that transfer from one situation to another. The fact that you coordinated a student organization, chaired meetings, supervised others, and managed a budget leads one to suspect that you could coordinate other things as well.

4. **Use descriptive job titles** that provide information about what you did. A "Student Intern" should be more specifically stated as, for example, "Magazine Operations Intern." "Volunteer" is also too general; a title like "Peer Writing Tutor" would be more appropriate.

5. **Create word pictures** by using active verbs to start sentences. Describe *results* you have produced in the work you have done.

A limp description would say something like the following: "My duties included helping with production, proofreading, and editing. I used a word processing package to alter text." An action statement would be stated as follows: "Coordinated and assisted in the creative marketing of brochures and seminar promotions, becoming proficient in WordPerfect."

Remember, an accomplishment is simply a result, a final measurable product that people can relate to. A duty is not a result, it is an obligation—every job holder has duties. For an effective resume, list as many results as you can. To make the most of the limited space you have and to give your description impact, carefully select appropriate and accurate descriptors from the list of action words in Exhibit 2.2.

Here are some traits that employers tell us they like to see:

❑ Teamwork

❑ Energy and motivation

❑ Learning and using new skills

❑ Demonstrated versatility

Exhibit 2.2

Resume Action Verbs

Achieved	Established	Operated
Acted	Estimated	Organized
Administered	Evaluated	Participated
Advised	Examined	Performed
Analyzed	Explained	Planned
Assessed	Facilitated	Predicted
Assisted	Finalized	Prepared
Attained	Generated	Presented
Balanced	Handled	Processed
Budgeted	Headed	Produced
Calculated	Helped	Projected
Collected	Identified	Proposed
Communicated	Illustrated	Provided
Compiled	Implemented	Qualified
Completed	Improved	Quantified
Composed	Increased	Questioned
Conceptualized	Influenced	Realized
Condensed	Informed	Received
Conducted	Initiated	Recommended
Consolidated	Innovated	Recorded
Constructed	Instituted	Reduced
Controlled	Instructed	Reinforced
Converted	Integrated	Reported
Coordinated	Interpreted	Represented
Corrected	Introduced	Researched
Created	Learned	Resolved
Decreased	Lectured	Reviewed
Defined	Led	Scheduled
Demonstrated	Maintained	Selected
Designed	Managed	Served
Determined	Mapped	Showed
Developed	Marketed	Simplified
Directed	Met	Sketched
Documented	Modified	Sold
Drafted	Monitored	Solved
Edited	Negotiated	Staffed
Eliminated	Observed	Streamlined
Ensured	Obtained	Studied

continued

continued		
Submitted	Tabulated	Updated
Summarized	Tested	Verified
Systematized	Transacted	

- Critical thinking

- Understanding how profits are created

- Displaying organizational acumen

- Communicating directly and clearly, in both writing and speaking

- Risk taking

- Willingness to admit mistakes

- Manifesting high personal standards

SOLUTIONS TO FREQUENTLY ENCOUNTERED PROBLEMS

Repetitive Employment with the Same Employer

EMPLOYMENT: The Foot Locker, Portland, Oregon. Summer 1991, 1992, 1993. Initially employed in high school as salesclerk. Due to successful performance, asked to return next two summers at higher pay with added responsibility. Ranked as the #2 salesperson the first summer and #1 the next two summers. Assisted in arranging eye-catching retail displays; served as manager of other summer workers during owner's absence.

A Large Number of Jobs

EMPLOYMENT: Recent Hospitality Industry Experience: Affiliated with four upscale hotel/restaurant complexes (September 1991–February 1994), where I worked part- and full-time as a waiter, bartender, disc jockey, and bookkeeper to produce income for college.

Several Positions with the Same Employer

EMPLOYMENT: Coca-Cola Bottling Co., Burlington, VT, 1991–94. In four years, I received three promotions, each with increased pay and responsibility.

Summer Sales Coordinator: Promoted to hire, train, and direct efforts of add-on staff of fifteen college-age route salespeople hired to meet summer peak demand for product.

Sales Administrator: Promoted to run home office sales desk, managing accounts and associated delivery schedules for professional sales force of ten people. Intensive phone work, daily interaction with all personnel, and strong knowledge of product line required.

Route Salesperson: Summer employment to travel and tourism industry sites using Coke products. Met specific schedule demands, used good communication skills with wide variety of customers, and demonstrated strong selling skills. Named salesperson of the month for July and August of that year.

QUESTIONS RESUME WRITERS OFTEN ASK

How Far Back Should I Go in Terms of Listing Past Jobs?

Usually, listing three or four jobs should suffice. If you did something back in high school that has a bearing on your future aspirations for employment, by all means list the job. As you progress through your college career, high school jobs may be replaced on the resume by college employment.

Should I Differentiate Between Paid and Nonpaid Employment?

Most employers are not initially concerned about how much you were paid. They are anxious to know how much responsibility you held in your past employment. There is no need to specify that your work was volunteer if you had significant responsibilities.

How Should I Represent My Accomplishments or Work-Related Responsibilities?

Succinctly, but fully. In other words, give the employer enough information to arouse curiosity, but not so much detail that you leave nothing to the imagination. Besides, some jobs merit more lengthy explanations than others. Be sure to convey any information that can give an employer a better understanding of the depth of your involvement at work. Did you supervise others? How many? Did your efforts result in a more efficient operation? How much did you increase efficiency? Did you handle a budget? How much? Were you promoted in a short time? Did you work two jobs at once or fifteen hours per week after high school? Where appropriate, quantify.

Should the Work Section Always Follow the Education Section on the Resume?

Always lead with your strengths. If your education closely relates to the employment you now seek, put this section after the objective. Or, if you are weak on the academic side but have a surplus of good work experiences, consider reversing the order of your sections to lead with employment, followed by education.

How Should I Present My Activities, Honors, Awards, Professional Societies, and Affiliations?

This section of the resume can add valuable information for an employer to consider if used correctly. The rule of thumb for information in this section is to include only those activities that are in some way relevant to the objective stated on your resume. If you can draw a valid connection between your activities and your objective, include them; if not, leave them out.

Granted, this is hard to do. Playing center on the championship basketball team or serving as coordinator of the biggest homecoming parade ever held are roles that have meaning for you and represent personal accomplishments you'd like to share. But the resume is a brief document, and the information you provide on it should help the employer make a decision about your job eligibility. Including personal details can be confusing and could hurt your candidacy. Limiting your activity list to a few very significant experiences can be very effective.

If you are applying for a position as a safety officer, your certificate in Red Cross lifesaving skills or CPR would be related and valuable. You would want to include it. If, however, you are applying for a job as a junior account executive in an advertising agency, that information would be unrelated and superfluous. Leave it out.

Professional affiliations and honors should *all* be listed; especially important are those related to your job objective. Social clubs and activities need not be a part of your resume unless you hold a significant office or you are looking for a position related to your membership. Be aware that most prospective employers' principal concerns are related to your employability, not your social life. If you have any, publications can be included as an addendum to your resume.

The focus of the resume is your experience and education. It is not necessary to describe your involvement in activities. However, if your resume needs to be lengthened, this section provides the freedom either to expand on or mention only briefly the contributions you have made. If you have made significant contributions (e.g., an officer of an organization or a particularly long tenure with a group), you may choose to describe them in more detail.

It is not always necessary to include the dates of your memberships with your activities the way you would include job dates.

There are a number of different ways in which to present additional information. You may give this section a number of different titles. Assess what you want to list, and then use an appropriate title. Do not use extracurricular activities. This terminology is scholastic, not professional, and therefore not appropriate. The following are two examples:

    ❑ ACTIVITIES: Society for Technical Communication, Student Senate, Student Admissions Representative, Senior Class Officer

    ❑ ACTIVITIES:
        • Society for Technical Communication Member
        • Student Senator
        • Student Admissions Representative
        • Senior Class Officer

The position you are looking for will determine what you should or should not include. *Always* look for a correlation between the activity and the prospective job.

How Should I Handle References?

The use of references is considered a part of the interview process, and they should never be listed on a resume. You would always provide references to a potential employer if requested to, so it is not even necessary to include this section on the resume if room does not permit. If space is available, it is acceptable to include one of the following statements:

    ❑ REFERENCES: Furnished upon request.

    ❑ REFERENCES: Available upon request.

Individuals used as references must be protected from unnecessary contacts. By including names on your resume, you leave your references unprotected. Overuse and abuse of your references will lead to less-than-supportive comments. Protect your references by giving out their names only when you are being considered seriously as a candidate for a given position.

THE FUNCTIONAL RESUME

The functional resume departs from a chronological resume in that it organizes information by specific accomplishments in various settings: previous

Exhibit 2.3

Functional Resume

WALTER A. ROBERTSON

621 Mary Street
Austin, TX 78767
(512) 555-7630 (voice)
(512) 555-8998 (fax)
E-mail: wrobertson@texmail.com

OBJECTIVE
An entry-level position teaching high school chemistry

CAPABILITIES
- Excellent instructional skills
- Outstanding oral communication skills
- Energetic and task-oriented
- Excellent quantitative and analytical skills
- Fluent in Spanish
- Experienced in working with young people
- Adept in use of computers

SELECTED ACCOMPLISHMENTS
YOUTH-ORIENTED ACTIVITY: Two years of experience as part-time youth worker for the City of Austin. Planned and implemented sports events and summer camp activities. Assisted in developing an after-school tutoring program.
SCIENCE ACTIVITIES: Extensive experience in working with high school students in science fair activities. Three years of experience as volunteer science fair coordinator for Johnson High School.
LEADERSHIP: Vice president, University of Texas Young Chemists Society. Publicity chairman, Student Government Association.

RECOGNITION/AWARDS
Departmental award, Outstanding Chemistry Undergraduate, 1998–99
Phi Lambda Beta Scholastic Honor Society, 1997–98
Dean's List, eight semesters

EMPLOYMENT HISTORY
Intern, Tri-State Chemicals, 1997
Youth Activities Counselor, Austin Recreation Department,
  1996–98

EDUCATION
Bachelor of Science, University of Texas, 1999
Major: Chemistry
Minor: Education
Certified grades 7–12

REFERENCES
Available on request.

---

jobs, volunteer work, associations, etc. This type of resume permits you to stress the substance of your experiences rather than the position titles you have held. (See Exhibit 2.3.) You should consider using a functional resume if you have held a series of similar jobs that relied on the same skills or abilities.

The Objective

A functional resume begins with an objective that can be used to focus the contents of the resume.

Specific Accomplishments

Specific accomplishments are listed on this type of resume. Examples of the types of headings used to describe these capabilities might include sales, counseling, teaching, communication, production, management, marketing, or writing. The headings you choose will directly relate to your experience and the tasks that you carried out. Each accomplishment section contains statements related to your experience in that category, regardless of when or where it occurred. Organize the accomplishments and the related tasks you describe in their order of importance as related to the position you seek.

Experience or Employment History

Your actual work experience is condensed and placed after the specific accomplishments section. It simply lists dates of employment, position titles, and employer names.

Education

The education section of a functional resume is identical to that of the chronological resume, but it does not carry the same visual importance because it is placed near the bottom of the page.

References

Because actual reference names are never listed on a resume, this section is optional if space does not permit.

THE TARGETED RESUME

The targeted resume focuses on specific work-related capabilities you can bring to a given position within an organization. (See Exhibit 2.4.) It should be sent to an individual within the organization who makes hiring decisions about the position you are seeking.

The Objective

The objective on this type of resume should be targeted to a specific career or position. It should be supported by the capabilities, accomplishments, and achievements documented in the resume.

Exhibit 2.4

Targeted Resume

JASON LYONS

462 Ash Place   755 Pleasant Drive
Cleveland, OH 44114   Columbus, OH 43229
(216) 555-0667   (614) 886-3349
(until May 1999)

JOB TARGET
An entry-level position in chemical sales or a related area

CAPABILITIES
- Excellent writer and speaker
- Self-starter with strong organizational skills
- Knowledgeable of chemical terms and concepts

- Familiar with a variety of computer software, including word processing software and spreadsheets

ACHIEVEMENTS
- Named "Sales Newcomer of the Year" as part-time sales associate, Smith Incorporated, Shaker Heights, Ohio
- Developed winning presentation in student marketing contest
- Developed/published my own Web page providing marketing tips for young people

WORK HISTORY
Summer 1998. Served internship at Allcar Chemicals, Cleveland, Ohio. Assisted in developing new product brochures. Helped plan new marketing program. Revised and improved company Web site. Provided general office support.
1996–98. Work-study student, Department of Natural Sciences, Case Western Reserve University, Cleveland, Ohio. Assisted department chairperson in general office duties. Also helped order and stock supplies for chemistry and biology laboratories.

EDUCATION
Earned Bachelor of Science in Chemistry
Case Western Reserve University
Completed minor in marketing

REFERENCES ON REQUEST

Capabilities

Capabilities should be statements that illustrate tasks you believe you are capable of based on your accomplishments, achievements, and work history. Each should relate to your targeted career or position. You can stress your qualifications rather than your employment history. This approach may require research to obtain an understanding of the nature of the work involved and the capabilities necessary to carry out that work.

Accomplishments/Achievements

This section relates the various activities you have been involved in to the job market. These experiences may include previous jobs, extracurricular activities at school, internships, and part-time summer work.

Experience

Your work history should be listed in abbreviated form and may include position title, employer name, and employment dates.

Education

Because this type of resume is directed toward a specific job target and an individual's related experience, the education section is not prominently located at the top of the resume as is done on the chronological resume.

THE BROADCAST LETTER

The broadcast letter is used by some job seekers in place of a resume and cover letter. (See Exhibit 2.5.) The purpose of this type of document is to

---

Exhibit 2.5

Broadcast Letter

LISA TWAIN
26 Paxon Street
Rumney, IL 60615
(812) 555-2955

Dr. Len Aldiss, Manager of Human Resources　　　　June 6, 1999
Wilson Chemicals
Box 448
Danvers, MA 29401

Dear Mr. Perkins,

　　I am writing to you because your organization may be in need of a sales professional with my education and experience. My long-term goal is to work in a sales management role, helping provide a high-quality sales and marketing program. Today's competitive business environment challenges us to provide high-level service to customers while at the same time preserving a strong "bottom line" orientation. I feel well prepared to contribute to your excellent sales team as they work hard to keep Wilson

Chemicals ahead of tomorrow's business challenges. Some highlights of my experience that might particularly interest you include:

- A serious interest in chemistry. I have majored in chemistry, earning excellent grades, and would now like to apply that knowledge in a business setting.

- My internship with a major chemical manufacturer provided me with a firsthand look at a modern business operation.

- As a part-time salesperson while in college, I have developed excellent customer relations skills as well as strong organizational and one-on-one communication skills.

- I have outstanding computer skills and am adept at various types of written communication.

I received my bachelor of science degree in chemistry from Black Mountain College in May of 1998.

It would be a pleasure to review my qualifications with you in a personal interview at some mutually convenient time. I will call your office at the end of next week to make arrangements. I look forward to discussing career opportunities with Wilson Chemicals.

Sincerely,

Lisa Twain

make a number of potential employers aware of the availability and expertise of the job seeker. Because the broadcast letter is mass-mailed (500 to 600 employers), the amount of work required may not be worth the return for many people. If you choose to mail out a broadcast letter, you can expect to receive a response from 2 to 5 percent, at best, of the organizations that receive your letter.

This type of document is most often used by individuals who have an extensive and quantifiable work history. College students often do not have the credentials and work experience to support using a broadcast letter, and most will find it difficult to effectively quantify a slim work history.

A broadcast letter is generally four paragraphs (one page) long. The first paragraph should immediately gain the attention of the reader and state some unusual accomplishment or skill that would be of benefit to the organization. It also states the reason for the letter. Details of the sender's work history are revealed in the third paragraph. These can appear in paragraph form or as a bulleted list. Education and other qualifications or credentials are then described. Finally, the job seeker indicates what he or she will do to follow up on the letter, which usually is a follow-up call one to two weeks after the letter is sent.

RESUME PRODUCTION AND OTHER TIPS

If you have the option and convenience of using a laser printer, you may want to initially produce a limited number of copies in case you want or need to make changes on your resume.

Resume paper color should be carefully chosen. You should consider the types of employers who will receive your resume and the types of positions for which you are applying. Use white or ivory paper for traditional or conservative employers or for higher-level positions.

Black ink on sharply white paper can be harsh on the reader's eyes. Think about an ivory or cream paper that will provide less contrast and be easier to read. Pink, green, and blue tints should generally be avoided.

Many resume writers buy packages of matching envelopes and cover sheet stationery that, although not absolutely necessary, does convey a professional impression.

If you'll be producing many cover letters at home, be sure you have high-quality printing equipment, whether it be computerized or standard typewriter equipment. Learn standard envelope formats for business and retain a copy of every cover letter you send out. You can use it to take notes of any telephone conversations that may occur.

If attending a job fair, women generally can fold their resume in thirds lengthwise and find it fits into a clutch bag or envelope-style purse. Both men and women will have no trouble if they carry a briefcase. For men without a briefcase, carry the resume in a nicely covered legal-size pad holder or fold it in half lengthwise and place it inside your suitcoat pocket, taking care it doesn't "float" outside your collar.

THE COVER LETTER

The cover letter provides you with the opportunity to tailor your resume by telling the prospective employer how you can be a benefit to the organization. It will allow you to highlight aspects of your background that are not already discussed in your resume and that might be especially relevant to the organization you are contacting or to the position you are seeking. Every resume should have a cover letter enclosed when you send it out. Unlike the resume, which may be mass-produced, a cover letter is most effective when it is individually typed and focused on the particular requirements of the organization in question.

A good cover letter should supplement the resume and motivate the reader to review the resume. The format shown in Exhibit 2.6 is only a suggestion to help you decide what information to include in writing a cover letter.

Begin the cover letter with your street address 12 lines down from the top. Leave three to five lines between the date and the name of the person to whom you are addressing the cover letter. Make sure you leave one blank line between the salutation and the body of the letter and between paragraphs.

Exhibit 2.6

Cover Letter Format

Your Street Address
Your Town, State, Zip
Phone Number
Date

Name
Title
Organization
Address

Dear _____:

First Paragraph. In this paragraph state the reason for the letter, name the specific position or type of work you are applying for, and indicate from which resource (career development office, newspaper, contact, employment service) you learned of the opening. The first paragraph can also be used to inquire about future openings.

Second Paragraph. Indicate why you are interested in the position, the company, its products or services, and what you can do for the employer. If you are a recent graduate, explain how

continued

continued

your academic background makes you a qualified candidate. Try not to repeat the same information found in the resume.

Third Paragraph. Refer the reader to the enclosed resume for more detailed information.

Fourth Paragraph. In this paragraph say what you will do to follow up on your letter. For example, state that you will call by a certain date to set up an interview or to find out if the company will be recruiting in your area. Finish by indicating your willingness to answer any questions they may have. Be sure you have provided your phone number.

Sincerely,

Type your name

Enclosure

After typing "Sincerely," leave four blank lines and type your name. This should leave plenty of room for your signature. A sample cover letter is shown in Exhibit 2.7.

The following guidelines will help you write good cover letters:

1. Be sure to type your letter; ensure there are no misspellings.

2. Avoid unusual typefaces, such as script.

3. Address the letter to an individual, using the person's name and title. To obtain this information, call the company. If answering a blind newspaper advertisement, address the letter "Good Morning" or omit the salutation.

4. Be sure your cover letter directly indicates the position you are applying for and tells why you are qualified to fill it.

5. Send the original letter, not a photocopy, with your resume. Keep a copy for your records.

6. Make your cover letter no more than one page.

7. Include a phone number where you can be reached.

Exhibit 2.7

Sample Cover Letter

13 Locust Street
San Diego, CA 98021
(619) 555-1111
October 12, 1998

Mr. Ken Kochien
Director of Research
West Coast Chemicals, Inc.
22 Main Street
Lockport, CA 98772

Dear Mr. Kochien:

In May of 1999 I will graduate from the San Diego campus of University College with a bachelor's degree in chemistry. I read of your opening for a chemist in *The Los Angeles Times*, and I am very interested in the possibilities it offers. I am writing to explore the opportunity for employment with West Coast Chemicals.

The advertisement indicated that you are looking for someone capable of conducting basic laboratory research in a self-directed fashion. I believe my resume outlines a work and education history that you will find interesting and relevant. Beginning with a part-time job in a local laboratory while in high school, I gained some research experience that was expanded by a special summer research program after my senior year. My college major has included a variety of theoretical courses as well as a great deal of laboratory experience, including two internships. I am a hard worker, focused, and capable of producing high-quality and thorough work under time constraints.

As you will see by the enclosed resume, I have had considerable laboratory experience here at college and am thoroughly familiar with all the equipment you mention in your ad. In addition, I have good research skills, and my computer skills are excellent.

I would like to meet with you to discuss how my education and experience would be consistent with your needs. I will contact your office next week to discuss the possibility of an interview. In

continued

continued

the meantime, if you have any questions or require additional information, please contact me at my home, (619) 555-1111.

Sincerely,

Mary Campbell
Enclosure

8. Avoid trite language and have someone read it over to react to its tone, content, and mechanics.

9. For your own information, record the date you send out each letter and resume.

CHAPTER THREE

RESEARCHING CAREERS

· ·

Many chemistry majors make their degree choice with the expectation that their degree would be the ticket to a job after graduation. But "chemistry" is a diverse field, populated with job titles you may never have considered. You know that pursuit of a chemistry major has given you an overview of the basic aspects of chemical interactions and various applications of research techniques. However, you still may be confused as to exactly what kinds of jobs you can do with your degree and what kinds of organizations will hire you. Are research jobs reserved only for chemistry majors who have earned advanced degrees? Where does a chemistry major fit into a corporation, state government agency, federal agency, or nonprofit organization?

· ·

WHAT DO THEY CALL THE JOB YOU WANT?

There is every reason to be unaware. One reason for confusion is perhaps a mistaken assumption that a college education provides job training. In most cases it does not. Of course, applied fields such as engineering, management, or education provide specific skills for the workplace, whereas most liberal arts degrees simply provide an education. A liberal arts education exposes you to numerous fields of study and teaches you quantitative reasoning, critical thinking, writing, and speaking, all of which can be successfully applied to a number of different job fields. But it still remains up to you to choose a job field and to learn how to articulate the benefits of your education in a way the employer will appreciate.

As indicated in Chapter 1 on self-assessment, your first task is to understand and value what parts of that education you enjoyed and were good at and would continue to enjoy in your life's work. Did your writing courses encourage you in your ability to express yourself in writing? Did you enjoy the research process, and did you find your work was well received? Did you enjoy any of your required quantitative subjects like algebra or calculus?

The answers to questions such as these provide clues to skills and interests you bring to the employment market over and above the credential of your degree. In fact, it is not an overstatement to suggest that most employers who demand a college degree immediately look beyond that degree to you as a person and your own individual expression of what you like to do and think you can do for them, regardless of your major.

COLLECTING JOB TITLES

The world of employment is a big place, and even seasoned veterans of the job hunt can be surprised about what jobs are to be found in what organizations. You need to become a bit of an explorer and adventurer and be willing to try a variety of techniques to begin a list of possible occupations that might use your talents and education. Once you have a list of possibilities that you are interested in and qualified for, you can move on to find out what kinds of organizations have these job titles.

Not every employer seeking to hire someone with a chemistry degree may be equally desirable to you. Some employment environments may be more attractive to you than others. A chemistry major considering government service could do that as an employee of a state agency, federal agency, or state-supported college or university. Though jobs might involve similar skills, each environment presents a different "culture" with associated norms in the pace of work, the interaction with others, and the background and training of those you'll work with or encounter on the job. Even in roles where job titles are quite similar, not all situations will present the same "fit" for you.

If you majored in chemistry and enjoyed the work you completed in laboratories, you might naturally think of working in a research position within a governmental agency or educational institution. But chemistry majors with similar skills and interests go on to work as researchers in the chemical industry, managers, and sales professionals and consultants, among other jobs. Some might go on to become teachers or professors. Each job title in this list can be found in a variety of settings.

....

Take training, for example. Trainers write policy and procedural manuals and actively teach to assist all levels of employees in mastering various tasks and work-related systems. Trainers exist in all large corporations, banks, consumer goods manufacturers, medical diagnostic equipment firms, sales organizations, and any organization that has processes or materials that need to be presented to and learned by the staff.

In reading job descriptions or want ads for any of these positions, you would find your four-year degree a "must." However, the academic major might be less important than your own individual skills in critical thinking, analysis, report writing, public presentations, and interpersonal communication. Even more important than thinking or knowing you have certain skills is your ability to express those skills concretely and the examples you use to illustrate them to an employer.

The best beginning to a job search is to create a list of job titles you might want to pursue, learn more about the nature of the jobs behind those titles, and then discover what kinds of employers hire for those positions. In the following section we'll teach you how to build a job title directory to use in your job search.

Developing a Job Title Directory That Works for You

A job title directory is simply a complete list of all the job titles you are interested in, are intrigued by, or think you are qualified for. Combining the understanding gained through self-assessment with your own individual interests and the skills and talents you've acquired with your degree, you'll soon start to read and recognize a number of occupational titles that seem right for you. There are several resources you can use to develop your list, including computer searches, books, and want ads.

Computerized Interest Inventories. One way to begin your search is to identify a number of jobs that call for your degree and the particular skills and interests you identified as part of the self-assessment process. There are excellent interactive computer career guidance programs on the market to help you produce such selected lists of possible job titles. Most of these are available at high schools and colleges and at some larger town and city libraries. Two of the industry leaders are SIGI and DISCOVER. Both allow you to enter interests, values, educational background, and other information to produce lists of possible occupations and industries. Each of the resources listed here will produce different job title lists. Some job titles will appear again and again, while others will be unique to a particular source. Investigate them all!

Reference Books. Books on the market that may be available through your local library, bookstore, or career counseling office also suggest various occupations related to a number of majors. The following are only two of the many good books on the market: *What Can I Do with a Major In . . . ? How to Choose and Use Your College Major,* by Lawrence R. Malnig with Anita Malnig, and *The Occupational Thesaurus. What Can I Do with a Major In . . . ?* lists job titles by academic major and identifies those jobs by their *Dictionary of Occupational Titles (DOT)* code. (See following discussion.)

· ·

For chemistry majors, a variety of job titles may be found in reference works listing occupational titles. In the *Dictionary of Occupational Titles,* for example, a look at major job categories can reveal other jobs. Under the heading for "Chemists" you might find different types of chemists, such as analytical chemists, food chemists, inorganic chemists, organic chemists, instrumentation chemists, and other types of chemists.

At the same time, you can also find some positions you may not have thought about. Their work is related to that of chemists, but duties differ. Position titles include chemical laboratory technician, chemical laboratory chief, chemical research engineer, chemical engineering technician, and chemical test engineer. Under other categories, such as "Teachers" or "Engineers," you may also find jobs related to chemistry. If a career in chemistry or a related field interests you, this source adds some depth by suggesting a number of different occupational directions.

....

Each job title deserves your consideration. Like the layers of an onion, the search for job titles can go on and on! As you spend time doing this activity, you are actually learning more about the value of your degree. What's important in your search at this point is not to become critical or selective, but rather to develop as long a list of possibilities as you can. Every source used will help you add new and potentially exciting jobs to your growing list.

Want Ads. It has been well publicized that newspaper want ads represent only about 10 to 15 percent of the current job market. Nevertheless, the Sunday want ads can be a great help to you in your search. Although they may not be the best place to look for a job, they can teach the job seeker much about the job market and provide a good education in job descriptions, duties and responsibilities, active industries, and some indication of the volume of job traffic. For our purposes they are a good source for job titles to add to your list.

Read the Sunday want ads in a major market newspaper for several Sundays in a row. Circle and then cut out any and all ads that interest you and seem to call for something close to your education and experience. Remember, because want ads are written for what an organization *hopes* to find, you don't have to meet absolutely every criterion. However, if certain requirements are stated as absolute minimums and you cannot meet them, it's best not to waste your time.

A recent examination of *The Boston Sunday Globe* reveals the following possible occupations for a liberal arts major with some computer skills and limited prior work experience. (This is only a partial list of what was available.)

- Admissions representative
- Salesperson
- Compliance director
- Assistant principal gifts writer
- Public relations officer
- Technical writer
- Personnel trainee
- GED examiner
- Direct mail researcher
- Associate publicist

After performing this exercise for a few Sundays, you'll find you have collected a new library of job titles.

The Sunday want ad exercise is important because these jobs are out in the marketplace. They truly exist, and people with your qualifications are being sought to apply. What's more, many of these advertisements describe the duties and responsibilities of the job advertised and give you a beginning sense of the challenges and opportunities such a position presents. Some will indicate salary, and that will be helpful as well. This information will better define the jobs for you and provide some good material for possible interviews in that field.

Exploring Job Descriptions

Once you've arrived at a solid list of possible job titles that interest you and for which you believe you are somewhat qualified, it's a good idea to do some research on each of these jobs. The preeminent source for such job information is the *Dictionary of Occupational Titles,* or *DOT*. This directory lists every conceivable job and provides excellent up-to-date information on duties and responsibilities, interactions with associates, and day-to-day assignments and tasks. These descriptions provide a thorough job analysis, but they do not consider the possible employers or the environments in which this job may be performed. So, although a position as a lab technician may be well defined in terms of duties and responsibilities, it does not explain the differences in doing lab work in a college or a hospital or an industrial setting. You will need to look somewhere else for work settings.

Learning More About Possible Work Settings

After reading some job descriptions, you may choose to edit and revise your list of job titles once again, discarding those you feel are not suitable and keeping those that continue to hold your interest. Or you may wish to keep your list intact and see where these jobs may be located. For example, if you are interested in lab work and you appear to have those skills and the requisite education, you'll want to know what organizations do lab work. How can you find that out? How much income does someone in lab work make a year and what is the employment potential for the field of lab work?

To answer these and many other good questions about your list of job titles, we recommend you try any of the following resources: *Careers Encyclopedia, Career Information Center, College to Career: The Guide to Job Opportunities,* and the *Occupational Outlook Handbook.* Each of these books, in a different way, will help to put the job titles you have selected into an employer context. *VGM's Handbook of Business and Management Careers* contains detailed career descriptions for more than fifty fields. Entries include complete information on duties and responsibilities for individual careers and detailed entry-level requirements. There is information on working conditions and promotional opportunities as well. Salary ranges and career out-look projections are also provided. Perhaps the most extensive discussion is found in the *Occupational Outlook Handbook,* which gives a thorough pre-sentation of the nature of the work, the working conditions, employment sta-tistics, training, other qualifications, and advancement possibilities as well as job outlook and earnings. Related occupations are also detailed, and a select bibliography is provided to help you find additional information.

Continuing with our lab work example, your search through these refer-ence materials would teach you that the lab-work–related jobs you find attractive are available with government agencies, colleges and universities, and corporations and small companies.

Networking to Get the Complete Story

You now have not only a list of job titles but also, for each of these job titles, a description of the work involved and a general list of possible employment settings in which to work. You'll want to do some reading and keep talking to friends, colleagues, teachers, and others about the possibilities. Don't neglect to ask if the career office at your college maintains some kind of alumni network. Often such alumni networks will connect you with another graduate from the college who is working in the job title or industry you are seeking information about. These career networkers offer what assistance they can. For some it is a full day "shadowing" the alumnus as he or she goes about the job. Others offer partial day visits, tours, informational interviews, resume reviews, job postings, or, if distance prevents a visit, telephone interviews. As fellow graduates, they'll be frank and informative about their own jobs and prospects in their field.

Take them up on their offer and continue to learn all you can about your own personal list of job titles, descriptions, and employment settings. You'll probably continue to edit and refine this list as you learn more about the realities of the job, the possible salary, advancement opportunities, and supply-and-demand statistics.

In the next section we'll describe how to find the specific organizations that represent these industries and employers so that you can begin to make contact.

WHERE ARE THESE JOBS, ANYWAY?

Having a list of job titles that you've designed around your own career interests and skills is an excellent beginning. It means you've really thought about who you are and what you are presenting to the employment market. It has caused you to think seriously about the most appealing environments to work in, and you have identified some employer types that represent these environments.

The research and the thinking that you've done this far will be used again and again. It will be helpful in writing your resume and cover letters, in talking about yourself on the telephone to prospective employers, and in answering interview questions.

Now is a good time to begin to narrow the field of job titles and employment sites down to some specific employers to initiate the employment contact.

Finding Out Which Employers Hire People Like You

This section will provide tips, techniques, and specific resources for developing an actual list of specific employers that can be used to make contacts. It is only an outline that you must be prepared to tailor to your own particular needs and according to what you bring to the job search. Once again, it is important to stress the need to communicate with others along the way exactly what you're looking for and what your goals are for the research you're doing. Librarians, employers, career counselors, friends, friends of friends, business contacts, and bookstore staff will all have helpful information on geographically specific and new resources to aid you in locating employers who'll hire you.

Identifying Information Resources

Your interview wardrobe and your new resume may have put a dent in your wallet, but the resources you'll need to pursue your job search are available for free (although you might choose to copy materials on a machine instead of taking notes by hand). The categories of information detailed here are not hard to find and are yours for the browsing.

Numerous resources described in this section will help you identify actual employers. Use all of them or any others that you identify as available in your geographic area. As you become experienced in this process, you'll quickly figure out which information sources are helpful and which are not. If you live in a rural area, a well-planned day trip to a major city that includes a college career office, a large college or city library, state and federal employment centers, a chamber of commerce office, and a well-stocked bookstore can produce valuable results.

There are many excellent resources available to help you identify actual job sites. They are categorized into employer directories (usually indexed by product lines and geographic location), geographically based directories (designed to highlight particular cities, regions, or states), career-specific directories (e.g., *Sports Market Place,* which lists tens of thousands of firms involved with sports), periodicals and newspapers, targeted job posting publications, and videos. This is by no means meant to be a complete list of resources, but rather a starting point for identifying useful resources.

Working from the more general references to highly specific resources, we will provide a basic list to help you begin your search. Many of these you'll find easily available. In some cases reference librarians and others will suggest even better materials for your particular situation. Start to create your own customized bibliography of job search references. Use copying services to save time and to allow you to carry away information about organization mission, location, company officers, phone numbers, and addresses.

Employer Directories. There are many employer directories available to give you the kind of information you need for your job search. Some of our favorites are listed here, but be sure to ask the professionals you are working with to make additional suggestions.

- ❑ *America's Corporate Families* identifies many major U.S. ultimate parent companies and displays corporate family linkage of subsidiaries and divisions. Businesses can be identified by their industrial code.

- ❑ *Million Dollar Directory: America's Leading Public and Private Companies* lists about 160,000 companies.

- ❑ *Moody's* various manuals are intended as guides for investors, so they contain a history of each company. Each manual contains a classification of companies by industries and products.

- ❑ *Standard and Poor's Register of Corporations* contains listings for 45,000 businesses, some of which are not listed in the *Million Dollar Directory.*

- ❑ *Job Seekers Guide to Private and Public Companies* profiles 15,000 employers in four volumes, each covering a different geographic region. Company entries include contact information, business descriptions, and application procedures.

- ❑ *The Career Guide: Dun's Employment Opportunities Directory* lists more than 5,000 large organizations, including hospitals and local governments. Profiles include an overview and history of the employer as well as opportunities, benefits, and contact names. It contains geographic and industrial indexes and indexes by discipline or internship availability. This guide also includes a state-by-state list of professional personnel consultants and their specialties.

❑ *Professional's Job Finder/Government Job Finder/Non-Profits Job Finder* are specific directories of job services, salary surveys, and periodical listings in which advertisements for jobs in the professional, government, or not-for-profit sector are found.

❑ *Opportunities in Nonprofit Organizations* is a VGM career series edition that opens up the world of not-for-profit by helping you match your interest profile to the aims and objectives of scores of nonprofit employers in business, education, health and medicine, social welfare, science and technology, and many others. There is also a special section on fund-raising and development career paths.

❑ *The 100 Best Companies to Sell For* lists companies by industry and provides contact information and describes benefits and corporate culture.

❑ *The 100 Best Companies to Work for in America* rates organizations on several factors including opportunities, job security, and pay.

❑ *Companies That Care* lists organizations that the authors believe are family-friendly. One index organizes information by state.

❑ *Infotrac CD-ROM Business Index* covers business journals and magazines as well as news magazines and can provide information on public and private companies.

❑ *ABI/Inform on Disc* (CD-ROM) indexes articles in more than 800 journals.

Geographically Based Directories. The Job Bank series published by Bob Adams, Inc. contains detailed entries on each area's major employers, including business activity, address, phone number, and hiring contact name. Many listings specify educational backgrounds being sought in potential employees. Each volume contains a solid discussion of each city's or state's major employment sectors. Organizations are also indexed by industry. Job Bank volumes are available for the following places: Atlanta, Boston, Chicago, Denver, Dallas–Ft. Worth, Florida, Houston, Ohio, St. Louis, San Francisco, Seattle, Los Angeles, New York, Detroit, Philadelphia, Minneapolis, the Northwest, and Washington, D.C.

National Job Bank lists employers in every state, along with contact names and commonly hired job categories. Included are many small companies often overlooked by other directories. Companies are also indexed by industry. This publication provides information on educational backgrounds sought and lists company benefits.

Career-Specific Directories. VGM publishes a number of excellent series detailing careers for college graduates. In the *Professional Career Series* are guides to careers in the following fields, among others:

- Advertising

- Communications

- Business

- Computers

- Health Care

- High Tech

Each provides an excellent discussion of the industry, educational requirements for jobs, salary ranges, duties, and projected outlooks for the field.

Another VGM series, *Opportunities In . . .,* has an equally wide range of titles relating to specific majors, such as the following:

- *Opportunities in Chemistry*

- *Opportunities in Engineering*

- *Opportunities in Federal Government*

- *Opportunities in Government Service*

- *Opportunities in Journalism*

- *Opportunities in Law*

- *Opportunities in State and Local Government*

- *Opportunities in Teaching*

- *Opportunities in Nonprofit Organizations*

Periodicals and Newspapers. Several sources are available to help you locate which journals or magazines carry job advertisements in your field. Other resources help you identify opportunities in other parts of the country.

- *Where the Jobs Are: A Comprehensive Directory of 1,200 Journals Listing Career Opportunities* links specific occupational titles to corresponding periodicals that carry job listings for your field.

- *Social & Behavioral Sciences Jobs Handbook* contains a periodicals matrix organized by academic discipline and highlights periodicals containing job listings.

❑ *National Business Employment Weekly* compiles want ads from four regional editions of the *Wall Street Journal.* Most are business and management positions.

❑ *National Ad Search* reprints ads from seventy-five metropolitan newspapers across the country. Although the focus is on management positions, technical and professional postings are also included. *Caution:* Watch deadline dates carefully on listings because deadlines may have already passed by the time the ad is printed.

❑ *The Federal Jobs Digest* and *Federal Career Opportunities* list government positions.

❑ *World Chamber of Commerce Directory* lists addresses for chambers worldwide, state boards of tourism, convention and visitors' bureaus, and economic development organizations.

This list is certainly not exhaustive; use it to begin your job search work.

Targeted Job Posting Publications. Although the resources that follow are national in scope, they are either targeted to one medium of contact (telephone), focused on specific types of jobs, or are less comprehensive than the sources previously listed.

❑ *Job Hotlines USA* pinpoints more than one thousand hard-to-find telephone numbers for companies and government agencies that use prerecorded job messages and listings. Very few of the telephone numbers listed are toll-free, and sometimes recordings are long, so callers beware!

❑ *The Job Hunter* is a national biweekly newspaper listing business, arts, media, government, human services, health, community-related, and student services job openings.

❑ *Current Jobs for Graduates* is a national employment listing for liberal arts professions, including editorial positions, management opportunities, museum work, teaching, and nonprofit work.

❑ *Environmental Opportunities* serves environmental job interests nationwide by listing administrative, marketing, and human resources positions along with education-related jobs and positions directly related to a degree in an environmental field.

❑ *Y National Vacancy List* shows YMCA professional vacancies, including development, administration, programming, membership, and recreation postings.

❑ *ARTSearch* is a national employment service bulletin for the arts, including administration, managerial, marketing, and financial management jobs.

❑ *Community Jobs* is an employment newspaper for the nonprofit sector that provides a variety of listings, including project manager, canvas director, government relations specialist, community organizer, and program instructor.

❑ *College Placement Council Annual: A Guide to Employment Opportunities for College Graduates* is an annual guide containing solid job-hunting information and, more importantly, displaying ads from large corporations actively seeking recent college graduates in all majors. Company profiles provide brief descriptions and available employment opportunities. Contact names and addresses are given. Profiles are indexed by organization name, geographic location, and occupation.

Videos. You may be one of the many job seekers who likes to get information via a medium other than paper. Many career libraries, public libraries, and career centers in libraries carry an assortment of videos that will help you learn new techniques and get information helpful in the job search. A small sampling of the multitude of videos now available includes the following:

❑ *The Skills Search* (20 min.) discusses three types of skills important in the workplace, how to present the skills in an interview, and how to respond to problem questions.

❑ *Effective Answers to Interview Questions* (35 min.) presents two real-life job seekers and shows how they realized the true meaning of interview questions and formulated positive answers.

❑ *Employer's Expectations* (33 min.) covers three areas that are important to all employers: appearance, dependability, and skills.

❑ *The Tough New Labor Market of the 1990s* (30 min.) presents labor market facts as well as suggestions on what job seekers should do to gain employment in this market.

❑ *Dialing for Jobs: Using the Phone in the Job Search* (30 min.) describes how to use the phone effectively to gain information and arrange interviews by following two new graduates as they learn and apply techniques.

Locating Information Resources

In recent years, both new and seasoned job seekers have learned that the job market is changing, and the old guarantees of lifelong employment no longer hold true. Some of our major corporations, which were once seen as the most prestigious of employment destinations, are now laying off thousands of employees. Middle management is especially hard hit in downsizing situations. On the other side of the coin, smaller, more entrepreneurial firms are adding employees and realizing enormous profit margins. The geography of the new job market is unfamiliar, and the terrain is much harder to map. New and smaller firms can mean different kinds of jobs and new job titles. The successful job seeker will keep an open mind about where he or she might find employment and what that employment might be called.

In order to become familiar with this new terrain, you will need to undertake some research, which can be done at any of the following locations:

- Public libraries

- Business organizations

- Employment agencies

- Bookstores

- Career libraries

Each one of these places offers a collection of resources that will help you get the information you need.

As you meet and talk with service professionals at all these sites, be sure to let them know what you're doing. Inform them of your job search, what you've already accomplished, and what you're looking for. The more people who know you're job seeking, the greater the possibility that someone will have information or know someone who can help you along your way.

Public Libraries. Large city libraries, college and university libraries, and even well-supported town library collections contain a variety of resources to help you conduct a job search. It is not uncommon for libraries to have separate "vocational choices" sections with books, tapes, and associated materials relating to job search and selection. Some are now even making resume creation software available for use by patrons.

Some of the publications we name throughout this book are expensive reference items that are rarely purchased by individuals. In addition, libraries carry a wide range of newspapers and telephone yellow pages as well as the usual array of books. If resources are not immediately available, many libraries have loan arrangements with other facilities and can make information available to you relatively quickly.

Take advantage of not only the reference collections, but also the skilled and informed staff. Let them know exactly what you are looking for, and they'll have their own suggestions. You'll be visiting the library frequently, and the reference staff will soon come to know who you are and what you're working on. They'll be part of your job search network!

Business Organizations. Chambers of Commerce, Offices of New Business Development, Councils on Business and Industry, Small Business Administration (SBA) offices, and professional associations can all provide geographically specific lists of companies and organizations that have hiring needs. They also have an array of other available materials, including visitors' guides and regional fact books that provide additional employment information.

These agencies serve to promote local and regional businesses and ensure their survival and success. Although these business organizations do not advertise job openings or seek employees for their members, they may be very aware of staffing needs among their member firms. In your visits to each of these locations, spend some time with the personnel getting to know who they are and what they do. Let them know of your job search and your intentions regarding employment. You may be surprised and delighted at the information they may provide.

Employment Agencies. Employment agencies (including state and federal employment offices), professional "headhunters" or executive search firms, and some private career counselors can provide direct leads to job openings. Don't overlook these resources. If you are mounting a complete job search program and want to ensure that you are covering the potential market for employers, consider the employment agencies in your territory. Some of these organizations work contractually with several specific firms and may have access that is unavailable to you. Others may be particularly well informed about supply and demand in particular industries or geographic locations.

In the case of professional (commercial) employment agencies, which include those executive recruitment firms labeled "headhunters," you should be cautious about entering into any binding contractual agreement. Before doing so, be sure to get the information you need to decide whether their services can be of use to you. Questions to ask include the following: Who pays the fee when employment is obtained? Are there any other fees or costs associated with this service? What is their placement rate? Can you see a list of previous clients and can you talk to any for references? Do they typically work with entry-level job seekers? Do they tend to focus on particular kinds of employment or industries?

A few cautions are in order, however, when you work with professional agencies. Remember, the professional employment agency is, in most cases, paid by the hiring organization. Naturally, their interest and attention is largely directed to the employer, not to the candidate. Of course, they want to provide good candidates to guarantee future contracts, but they are less interested in the job seeker than the employer.

For teacher candidates there are a number of good placement firms that charge the prospective teacher, not the employer. This situation has evolved over time as a result of supply and demand and financial structuring of most school systems, which cannot spend money on recruiting teachers. Usually these firms charge a nonrefundable administrative fee and, upon successful placement, require a fee based on percentage of salary, which may range from 10 to 20 percent of annual compensation. Often, this can be repaid over a number of months. Check your contract carefully.

State and federal employment offices are no-fee services that maintain extensive "job boards" and can provide detailed specifications for each job advertised and help with application forms. Because government employment application forms are detailed, keep a master copy along with copies of all additional documentation (resumes, educational transcripts, military discharge papers, proof of citizenship, etc.). Successive applications may require separate filings. Visit these offices as frequently as you can because most deal with applicants on a "walk-in" basis and will not telephone prospective candidates or maintain files of job seekers. Check your telephone book for the address of the nearest state and federal offices.

One type of employment service that causes much confusion among job seekers is the outplacement firm. Their advertisements tend to suggest they will put you in touch with the "hidden job market." They use advertising phrases such as "We'll work with you until you get that job" or "Maximize your earnings and career opportunities." In fact, if you read the fine print on these ads, you will notice these firms must state they are "Not an employment agency." These firms are, in fact, corporate and private outplacement counseling agencies whose work involves resume editing, counseling to provide leads for jobs, interview skills training, and all the other aspects of hiring preparation. They do this for a fee, sometimes in the thousands of dollars range, which is paid by you, the client. Some of these firms have good reputations and provide excellent materials and techniques. Most, however, provide a service you as a college student or graduate can receive free from your alma mater or through a reciprocity agreement between your college and a college or university located closer to your current address.

Bookstores. Any well-stocked bookstore will carry some job search books that are worth buying. Some major stores will even have an extensive section devoted to materials, including excellent videos, related to the job search process. Several possibilities are listed in the following sections. You will also find copies of local newspapers and business magazines. The one advantage that is provided by resources purchased at a bookstore is that you can read and work with the information in the comfort of your own home and do not have to conform to the hours of operation of a library, which can present real difficulties if you are working full time as you seek employment. A few minutes spent browsing in a bookstore might be a beneficial break from your job search activities and turn up valuable resources.

Career Libraries. Career libraries, which are found in career centers at colleges and universities and sometimes within large public libraries, contain a unique blend of the job search resources housed in other settings. In addition, career libraries often purchase a number of job listing publications, each of which targets a specific industry or type of job. You may find job listings specifically for entry-level positions for political science majors. Ask about job posting newsletters or newspapers specifically focused on careers in the area that most interests you. Each center will be unique, but you are certain to discover some good sources of jobs.

Most college career libraries now hold growing collections of video material on specific industries and on aspects of your job search process, including dress and appearance, how to manage the luncheon or dinner interview, how to be effective at a job fair, and many other specific titles. Some larger corporations produce handsome video materials detailing the variety of career paths and opportunities available in their organizations.

Some career libraries also house computer-based career planning and information systems. These interactive computer programs help you to clarify your values and interests and will combine that with your education to provide possible job titles and industry locations. Some even contain extensive lists of graduate school programs.

One specific kind of service a career library will be able to direct you to is computerized job search services. These services, of which there are many, are run by private companies, individual colleges, or consortiums of colleges. They attempt to match qualified job candidates with potential employers. The candidate submits a resume (or an application) to the service. This information (which can be categorized into hundreds of separate "fields" of data) is entered into a computer database. Your information is then compared with the information from employers about what they desire in a prospective employee. If there is a "match" between what they want and what you have indicated you can offer, the job search service or the employer will contact you directly to continue the process.

Computerized job search services can complement an otherwise complete job search program. They are *not*, however, a substitute for the kinds of activities described in this book. They are essentially passive operations that are random in nature. If you have not listed skills, abilities, traits, experiences, or education *exactly* as an employer has listed its needs, there is simply no match.

Consult with the staff members at the career libraries you use. These professionals have been specifically trained to meet the unique needs you present. Often you can just drop in and receive help with general questions, or you may want to set up an appointment to speak one-on-one with a career counselor to gain special assistance.

Every career library is different in size and content, but each can provide valuable information for the job search. Some may even provide some limited counseling. If you have not visited the career library at your college or alma mater, call and ask if these collections are still available for your use. Be sure to ask about other services that you can use as well.

If you are not near your own college as you work on your job search, call the career office and inquire about reciprocal agreements with other colleges that are closer to where you live. Very often your own alma mater can arrange for you to use a limited menu of services at another school. This typically would include access to a career library and job posting information and might include limited counseling.

CHAPTER FOUR

NETWORKING

Networking is the process of deliberately establishing relationships to get career-related information or to alert potential employers that you are available for work. Networking is critically important to today's job seeker for two reasons: it will help you get the information you need, and it can help you find out about *all* of the available jobs.

Getting the Information You Need

Networkers will review your resume and give you candid feedback on its effectiveness. They will talk about the job you are looking for and give you a candid appraisal of how they see your strengths and weaknesses. If they have a good sense of the industry or the employment sector for that job, you'll get their feelings on future trends in the industry as well. Some networkers will be very candid about salaries, job hunting techniques, and suggestions for your job search strategy. Many have been known to place calls right from the interview desk to friends and associates who might be interested in you. Each networker will make his or her own contribution, and each will be valuable.

Because organizations must evolve to adapt to current global market needs, the information provided by decision makers within various organizations will be critical to your success as a new job market entrant. Networking can help you find out about trends currently affecting the industries under your consideration.

Finding Out About All of the Available Jobs

Secondly, not every job that is available at this very moment is advertised for potential applicants to see. This is called the *hidden job market.* Only 15 to

20 percent of all jobs are formally advertised, which means that 80 to 85 percent of available jobs do not appear in published channels. Networking will help you become more knowledgeable about all the employment opportunities available during your job search period.

Although someone you might talk to today doesn't know of any openings within his or her organization, tomorrow or next week or next month an opening may occur. If you've taken the time to show an interest in and knowledge of their organization, if you've shown the company representative how you can help achieve organizational goals and that you can fit into the organization, you'll be one of the first candidates considered for the position.

Networking: A Proactive Approach

Networking is a proactive rather than a reactive approach. You, as a job seeker, are expected to initiate a certain level of activity on your own behalf; you cannot afford to simply respond to jobs listed in the newspaper. Being proactive means building a network of contacts that includes informed and interested decision makers who will provide you with up-to-date knowledge of the current job market and increase your chances of finding out about employment opportunities appropriate for your interests, experience, and level of education.

An old axiom of networking says "You are only two phone calls away from the information you need." In other words, by talking to enough people, you will quickly come across someone who can offer you help. Start with your professors. Each of them probably has a wide circle of contacts. In their work and travel they might have met someone who can help you or direct you to someone who can.

Control and the Networking Process

In deliberately establishing relationships, the process of networking begins with you in control—*you* are contacting specific individuals. As your network expands and you establish a set of professional relationships, your search for information or jobs will begin to move outside of your total control. A part of the networking process involves others assisting you by gathering information for you or recommending you as a possible job candidate. As additional people become a part of your networking system, you will have less knowledge about activities undertaken on your behalf; you will undoubtedly be contacted by individuals whom you did not initially approach. If you want to function effectively in surprise situations, you must be prepared at all times to talk with strangers about the informational or employment needs that motivated you to become involved in the networking process.

PREPARING TO NETWORK

In deliberately establishing relationships, maximize your efforts by organizing your approach. Five specific areas in which you can organize your efforts include reviewing your self-assessment, reviewing your research on job sites and organizations, deciding who it is you want to talk to, keeping track of all your efforts, and creating your self-promotion tools.

Review Your Self-Assessment

Your self-assessment is as important a tool in preparing to network as it has been in other aspects of your job search. You have carefully evaluated your personal traits, personal values, economic needs, longer-term goals, skill base, preferred skills, and underdeveloped skills. During the networking process you will be called upon to communicate what you know about yourself and relate it to the information or job you seek. Be sure to review the exercises that you completed in the self-assessment section of this book in preparation for networking. We've explained that you need to assess what skills you have acquired from your major that are of general value to an employer and to be ready to express those in ways employers can appreciate as useful in their own organizations.

Review Researching Job Sites and Organizations

In addition, individuals assisting you will expect that you'll have at least some background information on the occupation or industry of interest to you. Refer to the appropriate sections of this book and other relevant publications to acquire the background information necessary for effective networking. They'll explain how to identify not only the job titles that might be of interest to you, but also what kinds of organizations employ people to do that job. You will develop some sense of working conditions and expectations about duties and responsibilities—all of which will be of help in your networking interviews.

Decide Who It Is You Want to Talk To

Networking cannot begin until you decide who it is that you want to talk to and, in general, what type of information you hope to gain from your contacts. Once you know this, it's time to begin developing a list of contacts. Five useful sources for locating contacts are described here.

College Alumni Network. Most colleges and universities have created a formal network of alumni and friends of the institution who are particularly interested in helping currently enrolled students and graduates of their alma mater gain employment-related information.

•••

Because the chemistry major covers a broad spectrum of activity, you'll find chemistry majors employed in almost every sector of the economy—not only government, but also business and nonprofit. The diversity of employment, as evidenced by an alumni list from your college or university, should be encouraging to the chemistry graduate. Among such a diversified group, there are likely to be quite a few people you would enjoy talking with. Some might be working quite far from you, but that does not preclude a telephone call, letter, or E-mail message.

•••

It is usually a simple process to make use of an alumni network. You need only visit the alumni or career office at your college or university and follow the procedure that has been established. Often, you will simply complete a form indicating your career goals and interests and you will be given the names of appropriate individuals to contact. In many cases staff members will coach you on how to make the best use of the limited time these alumni contacts may have available for you.

Alumni networkers may provide some combination of the following services: day-long shadowing experiences, telephone interviews, in-person interviews, information on relocating to given geographic areas, internship information, suggestions on graduate school study, and job vacancy notices.

•••

What a valuable experience! If you are interested in a management position, you may be concerned about your degree preparation and whether you would be considered eligible to work in this field. Spending a day with an alumnus who works as an administrator for a research lab, asking questions about his or her educational preparation and training, will give you a more concrete view of the possibilities for your degree. Observing firsthand

how this person does the job and exactly what the job
entails is a far better decision criterion for you than just
reading on the subject could possibly provide.

....

Present and Former Supervisors. If you believe you are on good terms with
present or former job supervisors, they may be an excellent resource for providing information or directing you to appropriate resources that would have
information related to your current interests and needs. Additionally, these
supervisors probably belong to professional organizations, which they might
be willing to utilize to get information for you.

....

If, for example, you were interested in working as a
chemist for a plastics manufacturer and you are currently
working as a laboratory assistant at the university where
you earned your degree, talk with your supervisor or a
former professor. He or she will probably know at least
one contact in the plastics industry, or will know other
working chemists who have contacts in industry. At least
one of these people will probably be able to provide you
with names and telephone numbers of not only potential employers, but also currently employed chemists
working in the industrial setting. You could then begin
the networking process.

....

Employers in Your Area. Although you may be interested in working in a geographic location different from the one where you currently reside, don't overlook the value of the knowledge and contacts those around you are able to
provide. Use the local telephone directory and newspaper to identify the types
of organizations you are thinking of working for or professionals who have
the kinds of jobs you are interested in. Sometimes, a call made to a large
local employer for information on working in a particular field will yield more
pertinent information on training seminars, regional professional organizations, and potential employment sites than national organizations are willing
to provide.

Employers in Geographic Areas Where You Hope to Work. If you are thinking about relocating, identifying prospective employers or informational contacts in this new location will be critical to your success. Many resources are available to help you locate contact names. These include the yellow pages directory, the local newspapers, local or state business publications, and local chambers of commerce.

Professional Associations and Organizations. Professional associations and organizations can provide valuable information in several areas: career paths that you may not have considered, qualifications relating to those career choices, publications that list current job openings, and workshops or seminars that will enhance your professional knowledge and skills. They can also be excellent sources for background information on given industries: their health, current problems, and future challenges.

There are several excellent resources available to help you locate professional associations and organizations that would have information to meet your needs. Two especially useful publications are the *Encyclopedia of Associations* and the *National Trade and Professional Associations of the United States.*

Keep Track of All Your Efforts

It can be difficult, almost impossible, to remember all the details related to each contact you make during the networking process, so you will want to develop a record-keeping system that works for you. Formalize this process by using a notebook or index cards to organize the information you gather. Begin by creating a list of the people or organizations you want to contact. Record the contact's name, address, telephone number, and what information you hope to gain. Each entry might look something like this:

Contact Name	Address	Phone #	Purpose
Mr. Tim Keefe	Wrigley Bldg.		
Dir. of Mines	Suite 72	555-8906	Resume screen

Once you have created this initial list, it will be helpful to keep more detailed information as you begin to actually make the contacts. Using the Network Contact Record form in Exhibit 4.1, keep good information on all your network contacts. They'll appreciate your recall of details of your meetings and conversations, and the information will help you to focus your networking efforts.

Exhibit 4.1

Network Contact Record

Name: Be certain your spelling is absolutely correct.

Title: Pick up a business card to be certain of the correct title.

Employing organization: Note any parent company or subsidiaries.

Business mailing address: This is often different from the street address.

Business telephone number: Include area code/alternative numbers/fax/E-mail.

Source for this contact: Who referred you, and what is their relationship?

Date of call or letter: Use plenty of space here to record multiple phone calls or visits, other employees you may have met, names of secretaries/ receptionists, etc.

Content of discussion: Keep enough notes here to remind you of the substance of your visits and telephone conversations in case some time elapses between contacts.

Follow-up necessary to continue working with this contact: Your contact may request that you send him or her some materials or direct you to contact an associate. Note any such instructions or assignments in this space.

Name of additional networker: Here you would record the
Address: names and phone numbers of
Phone: additional contacts met at this
Name of additional networker: employer's site. Often you will
Address: be introduced to many people,
Phone: some of whom may indicate
Name of additional networker: a willingness to help in your
Address: job search.
Phone:

Date thank-you note written: May help to date your next contact.

Follow-up action taken: Phone calls, visits, additional notes.

continued

continued

Other miscellaneous notes: Record any other additional interaction you think may be important to remember in working with this networking client. You will want this form in front of you when telephoning or just before and after a visit.

Create Your Self-Promotion Tools

There are two types of promotional tools that are used in the networking process. The first is a resume and cover letter, and the second is a one-minute "infomercial," which may be given over the telephone or in person.

Techniques for writing an effective resume and cover letter are covered in Chapter 2. Once you have reviewed that material and prepared these important documents, you will have created one of your self-promotion tools.

The one-minute infomercial will demand that you begin tying your interests, abilities, and skills to the people or organizations you want to network with. Think about your goal for making the contact to help you understand what you should say about yourself. You should be able to express yourself easily and convincingly. If, for example, you are contacting an alumnus of your institution to obtain the names of possible employment sites in a distant city, be prepared to discuss why you are interested in moving to that location, the types of jobs you are interested in, and the skills and abilities you possess that will make you a qualified candidate.

To create a meaningful one-minute infomercial, write it out, practice it if it will be a spoken presentation, rewrite it, and practice it again if necessary until expressing yourself comes easily and is convincing.

Here's a simplified example of an infomercial for use over the telephone:

· ·

Hello, Mr. Harvey? My name is Carol Landis. I am a recent graduate of Gulf Coast College, and I wish to enter the sales field. I feel confident I have many of the skills I understand are valued for sales personnel in industrial settings. I have a strong chemistry background, as well as good computer skills. In addition, I have excellent interpersonal skills and am known as an energetic, self-motivated individual. I understand these are valuable traits in your line of work!

Mr. Harvey, I'm calling you because I still need more information about chemical sales and where I might fit in. I'm hoping you'll have time to sit down with me for about half an hour and discuss your perspective on careers in industrial sales with me. There are so many possible employers to approach, and I am seeking some advice on which might be the best bet for my particular combination of skills and experience.

Would you be willing to do that for me? I would greatly appreciate it. I am available most mornings, if that's convenient for you.

Other effective self-promotion tools include portfolios for those in the arts, writing professions, or teaching. Portfolios show examples of work, photographs of projects or classroom activities, or certificates and credentials that are job related. There may not be an opportunity to use the portfolio during an interview, and it is not something that should be left with the organization. It is designed to be explained and displayed by the creator. However, during some networking meetings, there may be an opportunity to illustrate a point or strengthen a qualification by exhibiting the portfolio.

BEGINNING THE NETWORKING PROCESS

Set the Tone for Your Contacts

It can be useful to establish "tone words" for any communications you embark upon. Before making your first telephone call or writing your first letter, decide what you want your contact to think of you. If you are networking to try to obtain a job, your tone words might include words like *genuine, informed,* and *self-knowledgeable.* When trying to acquire information, your tone words may have a slightly different focus, such as *courteous, organized, focused,* and *well-spoken.* Use the tone words you establish for your contacts to guide you through the networking process.

Honestly Express Your Intentions

When contacting individuals, it is important to be honest about your reasons for making the contact. Establish your purpose in your own mind and be able and ready to articulate it concisely. Determine an initial agenda, whether it be informational questioning or self-promotion, present it to your contact, and be ready to respond immediately. If you don't adequately prepare before initiating your contacts, you may find yourself at a disadvantage if you're asked to immediately begin your informational interview or self-promotion during the first phone conversation or visit.

Start Networking Within Your Circle of Confidence

Once you have organized your approach—by utilizing specific researching methods, creating a system for keeping track of the people you will contact, and developing effective self-promotion tools—you are ready to begin networking. The best place to begin networking is by talking with a group of people you trust and feel comfortable with. This group is usually made up of your family, friends, and career counselors. No matter who is in this inner circle, they will have a special interest in seeing you succeed in your job search. In addition, because they will be easy to talk to, you should try taking some risks in terms of practicing your information-seeking approach. Gain confidence in talking about the strengths you bring to an organization and the underdeveloped skills you feel hinder your candidacy. Be sure to review the section on self-assessment for tips on approaching each of these areas. Ask for critical but constructive feedback from the people in your circle of confidence on the letters you write and the one-minute infomercial you have developed. Evaluate whether you want to make the changes they suggest, then practice the changes on others within this circle.

Stretch the Boundaries of Your Networking Circle of Confidence

Once you have refined the promotional tools you will use to accomplish your networking goals, you will want to make additional contacts. Because you will not know most of these people, it will be a less comfortable activity to undertake. The practice that you gained with your inner circle of trusted friends should have prepared you to now move outside of that comfort zone.

It is said that any information a person needs is only two phone calls away, but the information cannot be gained until you (1) make a reasonable guess about who might have the information you need and (2) pick up the telephone to make the call. Using your network list that includes alumni, instructors, supervisors, employers, and associations, you can begin preparing your list of questions that will allow you to get the information you need. Review the question list shown below and then develop a list of your own.

Questions You Might Want to Ask

1. In the position you now hold, what do you do on a typical day?

2. What are the most interesting aspects of your job?

3. What part of your work do you consider dull or repetitious?

4. What were the jobs you had that led to your present position?

5. How long does it usually take to move from one step to the next in this career path?

6. What is the top position to which you can aspire in this career path?

7. What is the next step in *your* career path?

8. Are there positions in this field that are similar to your position?

9. What are the required qualifications and training for entry-level positions in this field?

10. Are there specific courses a student should take to be qualified to work in this field?

11. What are the entry-level jobs in this field?

12. What types of training are provided to persons entering this field?

13. What are the salary ranges your organization typically offers to entry-level candidates for positions in this field?

14. What special advice would you give a person entering this field?

15. Do you see this field as a growing one?

16. How do you see the content of the entry-level jobs in this field changing over the next two years?

17. What can I do to prepare myself for these changes?

18. What is the best way to obtain a position that will start me on a career in this field?

19. Do you have any information on job specifications and descriptions that I may have?

20. What related occupational fields would you suggest I explore?

21. How could I improve my resume for a career in this field?

22. Who else would you suggest I talk to, both in your organization and in other organizations?

Questions You Might Have to Answer

In order to communicate effectively, you must anticipate questions that will be asked of you by the networkers you contact. Review the list below and see if you can easily answer each of these questions. If you cannot, it may be time to revisit the self-assessment process.

1. Where did you get my name, or how did you find out about this organization?

2. What are your career goals?

3. What kind of job are you interested in?

4. What do you know about this organization and this industry?

5. How do you know you're prepared to undertake an entry-level position in this industry?

6. What course work have you taken that is related to your career interests?

7. What are your short-term career goals?

8. What are your long-term career goals?

9. Do you plan to obtain additional formal education?

10. What contributions have you made to previous employers?

11. Which of your previous jobs have you enjoyed the most, and why?

12. What are you particularly good at doing?

13. What shortcomings have you had to face in previous employment?

14. What are your three greatest strengths?

15. Describe how comfortable you feel with your communication style.

General Networking Tips

Make Every Contact Count. Setting the tone for each interaction is critical. Approaches that will help you communicate in an effective way include politeness, being appreciative of time provided to you, and being prepared and thorough. Remember, *everyone* within an organization has a circle of influence, so be prepared to interact effectively with each person you encounter in the networking process, including secretarial and support staff. Many information or job seekers have thwarted their own efforts by being rude to some individuals they encountered as they networked because they made the incorrect assumption that certain persons were unimportant.

Sometimes your contacts may be surprised at their ability to help you. After meeting and talking with you, they might think they have not offered much in the way of help. A day or two later, however, they may make a contact that would be useful to you and refer you to it.

With Each Contact, Widen Your Circle of Networkers. Always leave an informational interview with the names of at least two more people who can help you get the information or job that you are seeking. Don't be shy about asking for additional contacts; networking is all about increasing the number of people you can interact with to achieve your goals.

Make Your Own Decisions. As you talk with different people and get answers to the questions you pose, you may hear conflicting information or get conflicting suggestions. Your job is to listen to these "experts" and decide what information and which suggestions will help you achieve *your* goals. Only implement those suggestions that you believe will work for you.

SHUTTING DOWN YOUR NETWORK

As you achieve the goals that motivated your networking activity—getting the information you need or the job you want—the time will come to inactivate all or parts of your network. As you do so, be sure to tell your primary supporters about your change in status. Call or write to each one of them and give them as many details about your new status as you feel is necessary to maintain a positive relationship.

Because a network takes on a life of its own, activity undertaken on your behalf will continue even after you cease your efforts. As you get calls or are contacted in some fashion, be sure to inform these networkers about your change in status, and thank them for assistance they have provided.

Information on the latest employment trends indicates that workers will change jobs or careers several times in their lifetime. If you carefully and thoughtfully conduct your networking activities now, you will have solid experience when you need to network again.

CHAPTER FIVE

INTERVIEWING

*C*ertainly, there can be no one part of the job search process more fraught with anxiety and worry than the interview. Yet seasoned job seekers welcome the interview and will often say "Just get me an interview and I'm on my way!" They understand that the interview is crucial to the hiring process and equally crucial for them, as job candidates, to have the opportunity of a personal dialogue to add to what the employer may already have learned from a resume, cover letter, and telephone conversations.

Believe it or not, the interview is to be welcomed, and even enjoyed! It is a perfect opportunity for you, the candidate, to sit down with an employer and express yourself and display who you are and what you want. Of course, it takes thought and planning and a little strategy; after all, it *is* a job interview! But it can be a positive, if not pleasant, experience and one you can look back on and feel confident about your performance and effort.

For many new job seekers, a job, any job, seems a wonderful thing. But seasoned interview veterans know that the job interview is an important step for both sides—the employer and the candidate—to see what each has to offer and whether there is going to be a "fit" of personalities, work styles, and attitudes. And it is this concept of balance in the interview, that both sides have important parts to play, that holds the key to success in mastering this aspect of the job search strategy.

Try to think of the interview as a conversation between two interested and equal partners. You both have important, even vital, information to deliver and to learn. Of course, there's no denying the employer has some leverage, especially in the initial interview for recruitment or any interview scheduled by the candidate and not the recruiter. That should not prevent the interviewee from seeking to play an equal part in what should be a fair exchange of information. Too often the untutored candidate allows the interview to become one-sided. The employer asks all the questions and the candidate simply responds. The ideal would be for two mutually interested parties to sit down and discuss possibilities for each. For this is a *conversation of significance,* and it requires pre-interview preparation, thought about the tone of the interview, and planning of the nature and details of the information to be exchanged.

PREPARING FOR THE INTERVIEW

Most initial interviews are about thirty minutes long. Given the brevity, the information that is exchanged ought to be important. The candidate should be delivering material that the employer cannot discover on the resume and, in turn, the candidate should be learning things about the employer that he or she could not otherwise find out. After all, if you have only thirty minutes, why waste time on information that is already published? The information exchanged is more than just factual, and both sides will learn much from what they see of each other, as well. How the candidate looks, speaks, and acts is important to the employer. The employer's attention to the interview and awareness of the candidate's resume, the setting, and the quality of information presented are important to the candidate.

Just as the employer has every right to be disappointed when a prospect is late for the interview, looks unkempt, and seems ill-prepared to answer fairly standard questions, the candidate may be disappointed with an interviewer who isn't ready for the meeting, hasn't learned the basic resume facts, and is constantly interrupted for telephone calls. In either situation there's good reason to feel let down.

There are many elements to a successful interview, and some of them are not easy to describe or prepare for. Sometimes there is just a chemistry between interviewer and interviewee that brings out the best in both, and a good exchange takes place. But there is much the candidate can do to pave the way for success in terms of his or her resume, personal appearance, goals, and interview strategy—each of which we will discuss. However, none of this preparation is as important as the time and thought the candidate gives to personal self-assessment.

Self-Assessment

Neither a stunning resume nor an expensive, well-tailored suit can compensate for candidates who do not know what they want, where they are going, or why they are interviewing with a particular employer. Self-assessment, the process by which we begin to know and acknowledge our own particular blend of education, experiences, needs, and goals, is not something that can be sorted out the weekend before a major interview. Of all the elements of interview preparation, this one requires the longest lead time and cannot be faked.

Because the time allotted for most interviews is brief, it is all the more important for job candidates to understand and express succinctly why they are there and what they have to offer. This is not a time for undue modesty (or for braggadocio either); but it is a time for a compelling, reasoned statement of why you feel that you and this employer might make a good match. It means you have to have thought about your skills, interests, and attributes; related those to your life experiences and your own history of challenges and opportunities; and determined what that indicates about your strengths, preferences, values, and areas needing further development.

A common complaint of employers is that many candidates didn't take advantage of the interview time, didn't seem to know why they were there or what they wanted. When candidates are asked to talk about themselves and their work-related skills and attributes, employers don't want to be faced with shyness or embarrassed laughter; they need to know about you so they can make a fair determination of you and your competition. If you lose the opportunity to make a case for your employability, you can be certain the person ahead of you has or the person after you will, and it will be on the strength of those impressions that the employer will hire.

If you need some assistance with self-assessment issues, refer to Chapter 1. Included are suggested exercises that can be done as needed, such as making up an experiential diary and extracting obvious strengths and weaknesses from past experiences. These simple, pen-and-paper assignments will help you look at past activities as collections of tasks with accompanying skills and responsibilities. Don't overlook your high school or college career office. Many offer personal counseling on self-assessment issues and may provide testing instruments such as the Myers-Briggs Type Indicator (MBTI)®, the Harrington-O'Shea Career Decision Making® System (CDM), the Strong Interest Inventory (SII)®, or any of a wide selection of assessment tools that can help you clarify some of these issues prior to the interview stage of your job search.

The Resume

Resume preparation has been discussed in detail, and some basic examples of various types were provided. In this section we want to concentrate on how best to use your resume in the interview. In most cases the employer will have seen the resume prior to the interview, and, in fact, it may well have been the quality of that resume that secured the interview opportunity.

An interview is a conversation, however, and not an exercise in reading. So, if the employer hasn't seen your resume and you have brought it along to the interview, wait until asked or until the end of the interview to offer it. Otherwise, you may find yourself staring at the back of your resume and simply answering "yes" and "no" to a series of questions drawn from that document.

Sometimes an interviewer is not prepared and does not know or recall the contents of the resume and may use the resume to a greater or lesser degree as a "prompt" during the interview. It is for you to judge what that may indicate about the individual doing the interview or the employer. If your interviewer seems surprised by the scheduled meeting, relies on the resume to an inordinate degree, and seems otherwise unfamiliar with your background, this lack of preparation for the hiring process could well be a symptom of general management disorganization or may simply be the result of poor planning on the part of one individual. It is your responsibility as a potential employee to be aware of these signals and make your decisions accordingly.

• •

In any event, it is perfectly acceptable for you to get the conversation back to a more interpersonal style by saying something like "Mr. Smith, you might be interested in some recent experience I gained in an internship at a local corporation that is not detailed on my resume. May I tell you about it?" This can return the interview to two people talking to each other, not one reading and the other responding.

• •

By all means, bring at least one copy of your resume to the interview. Occasionally, at the close of an interview, an interviewer will express an interest in circulating a resume to several departments, and you could then offer to provide those. Sometimes an interview appointment provides an opportunity to meet others in the organization who may express an interest in you and your background, and it may be helpful to follow that up with a copy of your resume. Our best advice, however, is to keep it out of sight until needed or requested.

Appearance

Although many of the absolute rules that once dominated the advice offered to job candidates about appearance have now been moderated significantly, conservative is still the watchword unless you are interviewing in a fashion-related industry. For men, conservative translates into a well-cut dark suit with appropriate tie, hosiery, and dress shirt. A wise strategy for the male job seeker looking for a good but not expensive suit would be to try the men's department of a major department store. They usually carry a good range of sizes, fabrics, and prices; offer professional sales help; provide free tailoring; and have associated departments for putting together a professional look.

For women, there is more latitude. Business suits are still popular, but they have become more feminine in color and styling with a variety of jacket and skirt lengths. In addition to suits, better-quality dresses are now worn in many environments and, with the correct accessories, can be most appropriate. Company literature, professional magazines, the business section of major newspapers, and television interviews can all give clues about what is being worn in different employer environments.

Both men and women need to pay attention to issues such as hair, jewelry, and makeup; these are often what separates the candidate in appearance from the professional work force. It seems particularly difficult for the young job seeker to give up certain hair styles, eyeglass fashions, and jewelry habits, yet those can be important to the employer, who is concerned with your ability to successfully make the transition into the organization. Candidates often find the best strategy is to dress conservatively until they find employment. Once employed and familiar with the norms within your organization, you can begin to determine a look that you enjoy, works for you, and fits your organization.

Choose clothes that suit your body type, fit well, and flatter you. Feel good about the way you look! The interview day is not the best for a new hairdo, a new pair of shoes, or any other change that will distract you or cause you to be self-conscious. Arrive a bit early to avoid being rushed, and ask the receptionist to direct you to a restroom for any last-minute adjustments of hair and clothes.

Employer Information

Whether your interview is for graduate school admission, an overseas corporate position, or a lab position with a local company, it is important to know something about the employer or the organization. Keeping in mind that the interview is relatively brief and that you will hopefully have other interviews with other organizations, it is important to keep your research in proportion. If secondary interviews are called for, you will have additional time to do further research. For the first interview, it is helpful to know the organization's mission, goals, size, scope of operations, etc. Your research may uncover recent areas of challenge or particular successes that may help to fuel the interview. Use the "Where Are These Jobs, Anyway?" section of Chapter 3, your library, and your career or guidance office to help you locate this information in the most efficient way possible. Don't be shy in asking advice of these counseling and guidance professionals on how best to spend your preparation time. With some practice, you'll soon learn how much information is enough and which kinds of information are most useful to you.

INTERVIEW CONTENT

We've already discussed how it can help to think of the interview as an important conversation—one that, as with any conversation, you want to find pleasant and interesting and to leave you with a good feeling. But because this conversation is especially important, the information that's exchanged is critical to its success. What do you want them to know about you? What do you need to know about them? What interview technique do you need to particularly pay attention to? How do you want to manage the close of the interview? What steps will follow in the hiring process?

Except for the professional interviewer, most of us find interviewing stressful and anxiety-provoking. Developing a strategy before you begin interviewing will help you relieve some stress and anxiety. One particular strategy that has worked for many and may work for you is interviewing by objective. Before you interview, write down three to five goals you would like to achieve for that interview. They may be technique goals: smile a little more, have a firmer handshake, be sure to ask about the next stage in the interview process before leaving, etc. They may be content-oriented goals: find out about the company's current challenges and opportunities, be sure to speak of my recent research writing experiences or foreign travel, etc. Whatever your goals, jot down a few of them as goals for this interview.

Most people find that, in trying to achieve these few goals, their interviewing technique becomes more organized and focused. After the interview, the most common question friends and family ask is "How did it go?" With this technique, you have an indication of whether you met *your* goals for the meeting, not just some vague idea of how it went. Chances are, if you accomplished what you wanted to, it informed the quality of the entire interview. As you continue to interview, you will want to revise your goals to continue improving your interview skills.

Now, add to the concept of the significant conversation the idea of a beginning, a middle, and a closing and you will have two thoughts that will give your interview a distinctive character. Be sure to make your introduction warm and cordial. Say your full name (and if it's a difficult-to-pronounce name, help the interviewer to pronounce it) and make certain you know your interviewer's name and how to pronounce it. Most interviews begin with some "soft talk" about the weather, chat about the candidate's trip to the interview site, national events, etc. This is done as a courtesy to relax both you and the interviewer, to get you talking, and to generally try to defuse the atmosphere of excessive tension. Try to be yourself, engage in the conversation, and don't try to second-guess the interviewer. This is simply what it appears to be—casual conversation.

Once you and the interviewer move on to exchange more serious information in the middle part of the interview, the two most important concerns become your ability to handle challenging questions and your success at asking meaningful ones. Interviewer questions will probably fall into one of three categories: personal assessment and career direction, academic background, and knowledge of the employer. The following are some examples of questions in each category:

Personal Assessment and Career Direction

1. How would you describe yourself?

2. What motivates you to put forth your greatest effort?

3. In what kind of work environment are you most comfortable?

4. What do you consider to be your greatest strengths and weaknesses?

5. How well do you work under pressure?

6. What qualifications do you have that make you think you will be successful in this career?

7. Will you relocate? What do you feel would be the most difficult aspect of relocating?

8. Are you willing to travel?

9. Why should I hire you?

Academic Assessment

1. Why did you select your college or university?

2. What changes would you make at your alma mater?

3. What led you to choose your major?

4. What subjects did you like best and least? Why?

5. If you could, how would you plan your academic study differently? Why?

6. Describe your most rewarding college experience.

7. How has your college experience prepared you for this career?

8. Do you think that your grades are a good indication of your ability to succeed with this organization?

9. Do you have plans for continued study?

Knowledge of the Employer

1. If you were hiring a graduate of your school for this position, what qualities would you look for?

2. What do you think it takes to be successful in an organization like ours?

3. In what ways do you think you can make a contribution to our organization?

4. Why did you choose to seek a position with this organization?

The interviewer wants a response to each question but is also gauging your enthusiasm, preparedness, and willingness to communicate. In each response you should provide some information about yourself that can be related to the employer's needs. A common mistake is to give too much information. Answer each question completely, but be careful not to run on too long with extensive details or examples.

Questions About Underdeveloped Skills

Most employers interview people who have met some minimum criteria of education and experience. They interview candidates to see who they are, to learn what kind of personality they exhibit, and to get some sense of how this person might fit into the existing organization. It may be that you are asked about skills the employer hopes to find and that you have not documented. Maybe it's grant-writing experience, knowledge of the European political system, or a knowledge of the film world.

To questions about skills and experiences you don't have, answer honestly and forthrightly and try to offer some additional information about skills you do have. For example, perhaps the employer is disappointed you have no grant-writing experience. An honest answer may be as follows:

> No, unfortunately, I was never in a position to acquire those skills. I do understand something of the complexities of the grant-writing process and feel confident that my attention to detail, careful reading skills, and strong writing would make grants a wonderful challenge in a new job. I think I could get up on the learning curve quickly.

The employer hears an honest admission of lack of experience but is reassured by some specific skill details that do relate to grant writing and a confident manner that suggests enthusiasm and interest in a challenge.

For many students questions about their possible contribution to an employer's organization can prove challenging. Because your education has probably not included specific training for a job, you need to review your academic record and select capabilities you have developed in your major that an employer can appreciate. For example, perhaps you read well and can analyze and condense what you've read into smaller, more focused pieces. That could be valuable. Or maybe you did some serious research and you know you have valuable investigative skills. Your public speaking might be highly developed and you might use visual aids appropriately and effectively. Or maybe your skill at correspondence, memos, and messages is effective. Whatever it is, you must take it out of the academic context and put it into a new, employer-friendly context so your interviewer can best judge how you could help the organization.

Exhibiting knowledge of the organization will, without a doubt, show the interviewer that you are interested enough in the available position to have done some legwork in preparation for the interview. Remember, it is not necessary to know every detail of the organization's history, but rather to have a general knowledge about why it is in business and how the industry is faring.

Sometime during the interview, generally after the midway point, you'll be asked if you have any questions for the interviewer. Your questions will tell the employer much about your attitude and your desire to understand the organization's expectations so you can compare it to your own strengths. The following are some selected questions you might want to ask:

1. What are the main responsibilities of the position?

2. What are the opportunities and challenges associated with this position?

3. Could you outline some possible career paths beginning with this position?

4. How regularly do performance evaluations occur?

5. What is the communication style (meetings, memos, etc.) of the organization?

6. Describe a typical day for me in this position.

7. What kinds of opportunities might exist for me to improve my professional skills within the organization?

8. What have been some of the interesting challenges and opportunities your organization has recently faced?

Most interviews draw to a natural closing point, so be careful not to prolong the discussion. At a signal from the interviewer, wind up your presentation, express your appreciation for the opportunity, and be sure to ask what the next stage in the process will be. When can you expect to hear from them?

Will they be conducting second-tier interviews? If you're interested and haven't heard, would they mind a phone call? Be sure to collect a business card with the name and phone number of your interviewer. On your way out, you might have an opportunity to pick up organizational literature you haven't seen before.

With the right preparation—a thorough self-assessment, professional clothing, and employer information—you'll be able to set and achieve the goals you have established for the interview process.

CHAPTER SIX

NETWORKING OR INTERVIEWING FOLLOW-UP

Quite often there is a considerable time lag between interviewing for a position and being hired, or, in the case of the networker, between your phone call or letter to a possible contact and the opportunity of a meeting. This can be frustrating. "Why aren't they contacting me?" "I thought I'd get another interview, but no one has telephoned." "Am I out of the running?" You don't know what is happening.

CONSIDER THE DIFFERING PERSPECTIVES

Of course, there is another perspective—that of the networker or hiring organization. Organizations are complex with multiple tasks that need to be accomplished each day. Hiring is but one discrete activity that does not occur as frequently as other job assignments. The hiring process might have to take second place to other, more immediate organizational needs. Although it may be very important to you and it is certainly ultimately significant to the employer, other issues such as fiscal management, planning and product development, employer vacation periods, or financial constraints, may prevent an organization or individual within that organization from acting on your employment or your request for information as quickly as you or they would prefer.

USE YOUR COMMUNICATION SKILLS

Good communication is essential here to resolve any anxieties, and the responsibility is on you, the job or information seeker. Too many job seekers and networkers offer as an excuse that they don't want to "bother" the organization by writing letters or calling. Let us assure you here and now, once and for all, that if you are troubling an organization by over-communicating, someone will indicate that situation to you quite clearly. If not, you can only assume you are a worthwhile prospect and the employer appreciates being reminded of your availability and interest in them. Let's look at follow-up practices in both the job interview process and the networking situation separately.

FOLLOWING UP ON THE EMPLOYMENT INTERVIEW

A brief thank-you note following an interview is an excellent and polite way to begin a series of follow-up communications with a potential employer with whom you have interviewed and want to remain in touch. It should be just that—a thank you for a good meeting. If you failed to mention some fact or experience during your interview that you think might add to your candidacy, you may use this note to do that. However, this should be essentially a note whose overall tone is appreciative and, if appropriate, indicative of a continuing interest in pursuing any opportunity that may exist with that organization. It is one of the few pieces of business correspondence that may be handwritten, but always use plain, good quality, monarch-size paper.

If, however, at this point you are no longer interested in the employer, the thank-you note is an appropriate time to indicate that. You are under no obligation to identify any reason for not continuing to pursue employment with that organization, but if you are so inclined to indicate your professional reasons (pursuing other employers more akin to your interests, looking for greater income production than this employer can provide, a different geographic location than is available, etc.), you certainly may. It should not be written with an eye to negotiation for it will not be interpreted as such.

As part of your interview closing, you should have taken the initiative to establish lines of communication for continuing information about your candidacy. If you asked permission to telephone, wait a week following your thank-you note, then telephone your contact simply to inquire how things are progressing on your employment status. The feedback you receive here should be taken at face value. If your interviewer simply has no information, he or she will tell you so and indicate whether you should call again and when. Don't be discouraged if this should continue over some period of time.

If during this time something occurs that you think improves or changes your candidacy (some new qualification or experience you may have had), including any offers from other organizations, by all means telephone or write to inform the employer about this. In the case of an offer from a competing but less desirable or equally desirable organization, telephone your contact, explain what has happened, express your real interest in the organization, and inquire whether some determination on your employment might be made before you must respond to this other offer. If the organization is truly interested in you, they may be moved to make a decision about your candidacy. Equally possible is the scenario in which they are not yet ready to make a decision and so advise you to take the offer that has been presented. Again, you have no ethical alternative but to deal with the information presented in a straightforward manner.

When accepting other employment, be sure to contact any employers still actively considering you and inform them of your new job. Thank them graciously for their consideration. There are many other job seekers out there just like you who will benefit from having their candidacy improved when others bow out of the race. Who knows, you might at some future time have occasion to interact professionally with one of the organizations with whom you sought employment. How embarrassing to have someone remember you as the candidate who failed to notify them of taking a job elsewhere!

In all of your follow-up communications, keep good notes of who you spoke with, when you called, and any instructions that were given about return communications. This will prevent any misunderstandings and provide you with good records of what has transpired.

FOLLOWING UP ON THE NETWORK CONTACT

Far more common than the forgotten follow-up after an interview is the situation where a good network contact is allowed to lapse. Good communications are the essence of a network, and follow-up is not so much a matter of courtesy here as it is a necessity. In networking for job information and contacts, you are the active network link. Without you, and without continual contact from you, there is no network. You and your need for employment is often the only shared element between members of the network. Network contacts are made regardless of the availability of any particular employment. It is incumbent upon the job seeker, and common sense, that unless you stay in regular communication with the network, you will not be available for consideration should some job become available in the future.

This brings up the issue of responsibility, which is likewise very clear. The job seeker initiates network contacts and is responsible for maintaining those contacts; therefore, the entire responsibility for the network belongs with him or her. This becomes patently obvious if the network is left unattended. It very shortly falls out of existence because it cannot survive without careful attention by the networker.

A variety of ways are available to you to keep the lines of communication open and to attempt to interest the network in you as a possible employee. You are limited only by your own enthusiasm for members of the network and your creativity. However, you as a networker are well advised to keep good records of whom you have met and spoken with in each organization. Be sure to send thank-you notes to anyone who has spent any time with you, be it a quick tour of a department or a sit-down informational interview. All of these communications should, in addition to their ostensible reason, add some information about you and your particular combination of strengths and attributes.

You can contact your network at any time to convey continued interest, to comment on some recent article you came across concerning an organization, to add information about your training or changes in your qualifications, to ask advice or seek guidance in your job search, or to request referrals to other possible network opportunities. Sometimes just a simple note to network members reminding them of your job search, indicating that you have been using their advice, and noting that you are still actively pursuing leads and hope to continue to interact with them is enough to keep communications alive.

Because networks have been abused in the past, it's important that your conduct be above reproach. Networks are exploratory options; they are not back-door access to employers. The network works best for someone who is exploring a new industry or making a transition into a new area of employment and who needs to find information or to alert people to his or her search activity. Always be candid and direct with contacts in expressing the purpose of your call or letter and your interest in their help or information about their organization. In follow-up contacts keep the tone professional and direct. Your honesty will be appreciated, and people will respond as best they can if your qualifications appear to meet their forthcoming needs. The network does not owe you anything, and that tone should be clear to each person you meet.

FEEDBACK FROM FOLLOW-UPS

A network contact may prove to be miscalculated. Perhaps you were referred to someone and it became clear that your goals and his or her particular needs did not make a good match. Or the network contact may simply not be in a position to provide you with the information you are seeking. Or in some unfortunate situations, the contact may become annoyed by being contacted for this purpose. In such a situation, many job seekers simply say "Thank you" and move on.

If the contact is simply not the right contact, but the individual you are speaking with is not annoyed by the call, it might be a better tactic to express regret that the contact was misplaced and then express to the contact what you are seeking and ask for his or her advice or possible suggestions as to a next step. The more people who are aware you are seeking employment, the better your chances of connecting, and that is the purpose of a network. Most people in a profession have excellent knowledge of their field and varying amounts of expertise on areas near to or tangent to their own. Use their expertise and seek some guidance before you dissolve the contact. You may be pleasantly surprised.

Occasionally, networkers will express the feeling that they have done as much as they can or provided all the information that is available to them. This may be a cue that they would like to be released from your network. Be alert to such attempts to terminate, graciously thank the individual by letter, and move on in your network development. A network is always changing, adding and losing members, and you want the network to be composed only of those who are actively interested in supporting your interests.

A FINAL POINT ON NETWORKING FOR CHEMISTRY MAJORS

In almost any area a chemistry major might consider as a potential career path, your contacts will be critically evaluating all your written and oral communications. For some job seekers, this may be more crucial than others. Many of the jobs in the career paths that follow do, however, require good communication skills. This should be a welcome demand, as your college studies have involved writing essays and research papers, as well as some classroom presentations—all of which have helped polish your communication style.

In your telephone communications, interview presentations, and follow-up correspondence, your written and spoken use of English will be part of the portfolio of impressions you create in those you meet along the way.

CHAPTER SEVEN

JOB OFFER CONSIDERATIONS

for many recent college graduates, the thrill of their first job and, for some, the most substantial regular income they have ever earned seems an excess of good fortune coming at once. To question that first income or be critical in any way of the conditions of employment at the time of the initial offer seems like looking a gift horse in the mouth. It doesn't seem to occur to many new hires even to attempt to negotiate any aspect of their first job. And, as many employers who deal with entry-level jobs for recent college graduates will readily confirm, the reality is that there simply isn't much movement in salary available to these new college recruits. The entry-level hire generally does not have an employment track record on a professional level to provide any leverage for negotiation. Real negotiations on salary, benefits, retirement provisions, etc., come to those with significant employment records at higher income levels.

Of course, the job offer is more than just money. It can be comprised of geographic assignment, duties and responsibilities, training, benefits, health and medical insurance, educational assistance, car allowance or company vehicle, and a host of other items. All of this is generally detailed in the formal letter that presents the final job offer. In most cases this is a follow-up to a personal phone call from the employer representative who has been principally responsible for your hiring process.

That initial telephone offer is certainly binding as a verbal agreement, but most firms follow up with a detailed letter outlining the most significant parts of your employment contract. You may certainly choose to respond immediately at the time of the telephone offer (which would be considered a binding oral contract), but you will also be required to formally answer the letter of offer with a letter of acceptance, restating the salient elements of the employer's description of your position, salary, and benefits. This ensures that both parties are clear on the terms and conditions of employment and remuneration and any other outstanding aspects of the job offer.

IS THIS THE JOB YOU WANT?

Most new employees will write this letter of acceptance back, glad to be in the position to accept employment. If you've worked hard to get the offer and the job market is tight, other offers may not be in sight, so you will say "Yes, I accept!" What is important here is that the job offer you accept be one that does fit your particular needs, values, and interests as you've outlined them in your self-assessment process. Moreover, it should be a job that will not only use your skills and education, but also challenge you to develop new skills and talents.

Jobs are sometimes accepted too hastily, for the wrong reasons, and without proper scrutiny by the applicant. For example, an individual might readily accept a sales job only to find the continual rejection by potential clients unendurable. An office worker might realize within weeks the constraints of a desk job and yearn for more activity. Employment is an important part of our lives. It is, for most of our adult lives, our most continuous productive activity. We want to make good choices based on the right criteria.

If you have a low tolerance for risk, a job based on commission will certainly be very anxiety provoking. If being near your family is important, issues of relocation could present a decision crisis for you. If you're an adventurous person, a job with frequent travel would provide needed excitement and be very desirable. The importance of income, the need to continue your education, your personal health situation—all of these have an impact on whether the job you are considering will ultimately meet your needs. Unless you've spent some time understanding and thinking about these issues, it will be difficult to evaluate offers you do receive.

More importantly, if you make a decision that you cannot tolerate and feel you must leave that job, you will then have both unemployment and self-esteem issues to contend with. These will combine to make the next job search tough going, indeed. So make your acceptance a carefully considered decision.

NEGOTIATING YOUR OFFER

It may be that there is some aspect of your job offer that is not particularly attractive to you. Perhaps there is no relocation allotment to help you move your possessions, and this presents some financial hardship for you. It may be that the medical and health insurance is less than you had hoped. Your initial assignment may be different than you expected, either in its location or in the duties and responsibilities that comprise it. Or it may simply be that the salary is less than you anticipated. Other considerations may be your official starting date of employment, vacation time, evening hours, dates of training programs or schools, etc.

If you are considering not accepting the job because of some item or items in the job offer "package" that do not meet your needs, you should know that most employers emphatically wish that you would bring that issue to their attention. It may be that the employer can alter it to make the offer more agreeable for you. In some cases it cannot be changed. In any event the employer would generally like to have the opportunity to try to remedy a difficulty rather than risk losing a good potential employee over an issue that might have been resolved. After all, they have spent time and funds in securing your services, and they certainly deserve an opportunity to resolve any possible differences.

Honesty is the best approach in discussing any objections or uneasiness you might have over the employer's offer. Having received your formal offer in writing, contact your employer representative and indicate your particular dissatisfaction in a straightforward manner. For example, you might explain that, while very interested in being employed by this organization, the salary (or any other benefit) is less than you have determined you require. State the terms you do need, and listen to the response. You may be asked to put this in writing, or you may be asked to hold off until the firm can decide on a response. If you are dealing with a senior representative of the organization, one who has been involved in hiring for some time, you may get an immediate response or a solid indication of possible outcomes.

Perhaps the issue is one of relocation. Your initial assignment is in the Midwest, and because you had indicated a strong West Coast preference, you are surprised at the actual assignment. You might simply indicate that, while you understand the need for the company to assign you based on its needs, you are disappointed and had hoped to be placed on the West Coast. You could inquire if that were still possible and, if not, would it be reasonable to expect a West Coast relocation in the future.

If your request is presented in a reasonable way, most employers will not see this as jeopardizing your offer. If they can agree to your proposal, they will. If not, they will simply tell you so, and you may choose to continue your candidacy with them or remove yourself from consideration as a possible employee. The choice will be up to you.

Some firms will adjust benefits within their parameters to meet the candidate's need if at all possible. If a candidate requires a relocation cost allowance, he or she may be asked to forgo tuition benefits for the first year to accomplish this adjustment. An increase in life insurance may be adjusted by some other benefit trade off; perhaps a family dental plan is not needed. In these decisions you are called upon, sometimes under time pressure, to know how you value these issues and how important each is to you.

Many employers find they are more comfortable negotiating for candidates who have unique qualifications or who bring especially needed expertise to the organization. Employers hiring large numbers of entry-level college graduates may be far more reluctant to accommodate any changes in offer conditions. They are well supplied with candidates with similar education and experience, so that if rejected by one candidate, they can draw new candidates from an ample labor pool.

COMPARING OFFERS

With only about 40 percent of recent college graduates employed three months after graduation, many graduates do not get to enjoy the experience of entertaining more than one offer at a time. The conditions of the economy, the job seekers' particular geographic job market, and their own needs and demands for certain employment conditions may not provide more than one offer at a time. Some job seekers may feel that no reasonable offer should go unaccepted for the simple fear there won't be another.

In a tough job market, or if the job you seek is not widely available, or when your job search goes on too long and becomes difficult to sustain financially and emotionally, it may be necessary to accept an offer. The alternative is continued unemployment. Even here, when you feel you don't have a choice, you can at least understand that in accepting this particular offer, there may be limitations and conditions you don't appreciate. At the time of acceptance, there were no other alternatives, but the new employee can begin to use that position to gain the experience and talent to move toward a more attractive position.

Sometimes, however, more than one offer is received at one time, and the candidate has the luxury of choice. If the job seeker knows what he or she wants and has done the necessary self-assessment honestly and thoroughly, it may be clear that one of the offers conforms more closely to those expressed wants and needs.

However, if, as so often happens, the offers are similar in terms of conditions and salary, the question then becomes which organization might provide the necessary climate, opportunities, and advantages for your professional development and growth. This is the time when solid employer research and astute questioning during the interviews really pays off. How much did you learn about the employer through your own research and skillful questioning?

When the interviewer asked during the interview "Do you have any questions?" did you ask the kinds of questions that would help resolve a choice between one organization and another? Just as an employer must decide among numerous applicants, so must the applicant learn to assess the potential employer. Both are partners in the job search.

RENEGING ON AN OFFER

An especially disturbing occurrence for employers and career counseling professionals is when a job seeker formally (either orally or by written contract) accepts employment with one organization and later reneges on the agreement and goes with another employer.

There are all kinds of rationalizations offered for this unethical behavior. None of them satisfies. The sad irony is that what the job seeker is willing to do to the employer—make a promise and then break it—he or she would be outraged to have done to them—have the job offer pulled. It is a very bad way to begin a career. It suggests the individual has not taken the time to do the necessary self-assessment and self-awareness exercises to think and judge critically. The new offer taken may, in fact, be no better or worse than the one refused. Job candidates should be aware that there have been incidents of legal action following job candidates reneging on an offer. This adds a very sour note to what should be a harmonious beginning of a lifelong adventure.

CHAPTER EIGHT

THE GRADUATE SCHOOL CHOICE

T he reasons for continuing one's education in graduate school can be as varied and unique as the individuals electing this course of action. Many continue their studies at an advanced level because they simply find it difficult to end the educational process. They love what they are learning and want to learn more and continue their academic exploration.

• •

Continuing to work with a particular subject, such as the way low temperatures affect chemical processes; and thinking, studying, and conducting laboratory research can provide excitement, challenge, and serious work. Some chemistry majors have loved this aspect of their academic work and want to continue that activity.

Others go on to graduate school for purely practical reasons. They have examined employment prospects in their field of study, and all indications are that a graduate degree is required. Or they sense opportunities to work at the level they prefer in government, industry, or education would be limited without a master's or doctorate.

Alumni who are working in the fields you are considering can be a good source of information as to the degree level the field demands. Ask your college career office for some alumni names, and give those people a call. Prepare some questions on specific job prospects in their field at each degree level. A thorough examination of the marketplace and talking to employers and professors will give you a sense of the scope of employment for a bachelor's, master's, or doctoral degree in chemistry or related fields.

College teaching will require an advanced degree. The same is true of most senior-level research positions, as well as many science management positions. Many of the career paths outlined in this book will require advanced education and perhaps some particular specialization in a subject area (such as analytic chemistry or biochemistry).

CONSIDER YOUR MOTIVES

The answer to the question of "Why graduate school?" is a personal one for each applicant. Nevertheless, it is important to consider your motives carefully. Graduate school involves additional time out of the employment market, a high degree of critical evaluation, significant autonomy as you pursue your studies, and considerable financial expenditure. For some students in doctoral programs, there may be additional life choice issues, such as relationships, marriage, and parenthood, that may present real challenges while in a program of study. You would be well-advised to consider the following questions as you think about your decision to continue your studies.

Are You Postponing Some Tough Decisions by Going to School?
Graduate school is not a place to go to avoid life's problems. There is intense competition for graduate school slots and for the fellowships, scholarships, and financial aid available. This competition means extensive interviewing, resume submission, and essay writing that rivals corporate recruitment. Likewise, the graduate school process is a mentored one in which faculty stay aware of and involved in the academic progress of their students and continually challenge the quality of their work. Many graduate students are called upon to participate in teaching and professional writing and research as well.

In other words, this is no place to hide from the spotlight. Graduate students work very hard and much is demanded of them individually. If you elect to go to graduate school to avoid the stresses and strains of the "real world," you will find no safe place in higher academics. Vivid accounts, both fiction and nonfiction, have depicted quite accurately the personal and professional demands of graduate school work.

The selection of graduate studies as a career option should be a positive choice—something you *want* to do. It shouldn't be selected as an escape from other, less attractive or more challenging options, nor should it be selected as the option of last resort (i.e., "I can't do anything else; I'd better just stay in school."). If you're in some doubt about the strength of your reasoning about continuing in school, discuss the issues with a career counselor. Together you can clarify your reasoning, and you'll get some sound feedback on what you're about to undertake.

On the other hand, staying on in graduate school because of a particularly poor employment market and a lack of jobs at entry-level positions has proved to be an effective "stalling" strategy. If you can afford it, pursuing a graduate degree immediately after your undergraduate education gives you a year or two to "wait out" a difficult economic climate while at the same time acquiring a potentially valuable credential.

Have You Done Some "Hands-On" Reality Testing?

There are experiential options available to give some reality to your decision-making process about graduate school. Internships or work in the field can give you a good idea about employment demands, conditions, and atmosphere.

· ·

A master's degree, or more typically a doctoral degree, is a frequent choice of chemistry majors who hope to advance their careers. You'll want to read Chapters 10 through 13 in this book to understand how you can make the most of both your graduate education and your career. Publications such as *The Chronicle of Higher Education* contain information that can provide background information on graduate studies and their applications.

For chemistry majors who want to take their graduate education to the doctoral level, with an eye to research or college teaching, the need for some hands-on reality testing is vital. Begin with your own college professors and ask them to talk to you about their own educational and career paths that have taken them to their current teaching posts. They will have had actual experience and inside information regarding the current market for Ph.D.s in chemistry.

Whether it's a master's or a Ph.D. in chemistry that is in your future, the kind of reality tests that come through internships, part-time jobs, and, most importantly, talking to people who have attained the kinds of careers you are seeking, will give you the best kind of information to make your decision.

....

Do You Need an Advanced Degree to Work in Your Field?

Certainly there are fields such as law, psychiatry, medicine, and college teaching that demand advanced degrees. Is the field of employment you're considering one that also puts a premium on an advanced degree? You may be surprised. Read the want ads in a number of major Sunday newspapers for positions you would enjoy. How many of those require an advanced degree?

Retailing, for example, has always put a premium on what people can do, rather than how much education they have had. Successful people in retailing come from all academic preparations. A Ph.D. in English may bring only prestige to the individual employed as a magazine researcher. It may not bring a more senior position or better pay. In fact, it may disqualify you for some jobs because an employer might believe you will be unhappy to be overqualified for a particular position. Or your motives in applying for the work may be misconstrued, and the employer might think you will only be working at this level until something better comes along. None of this may be true for you, but it comes about because you are working outside of the usual territory for that degree level.

When economic times are especially difficult, we tend to see stories featured about individuals with advanced degrees doing what is considered unsuitable work, such as the Ph.D. in English driving a cab or the Ph.D. in chemistry waiting tables. Actually, this is not particularly surprising when you consider that as your degree level advances, the job market narrows appreciably. At any one time, regardless of economic circumstances, there are only so many jobs for your particular level of expertise. If you cannot find employment for your advanced degree level, chances are you will be considered suspect for many other kinds of employment and may be forced into temporary work far removed from your original intention.

Before making an important decision such as graduate study, learn your options and carefully consider what you want to do with your advanced degree.

Ask yourself whether it is reasonable to think you can achieve your goals. Will there be jobs when you graduate? Where will they be? What will they pay? How competitive will the market be at that time, based on current predictions?

If you're uncertain about the degree requirements for the fields you're interested in, you should check a publication such as the U.S. Department of Labor's *Occupational Outlook Handbook*. Each entry has a section on training and other qualifications that will indicate clearly what the minimum educational requirement is for employment, what degree is the standard, and what employment may be possible without the required credential.

For example, for physicists and astronomers, a doctoral degree in physics or a closely related field is essential. Certainly this is the degree of choice in academic institutions. However, the *Occupational Outlook Handbook* also indicates what kinds of employment may be available to individuals holding a master's or even a bachelor's degree in physics.

Have You Compared Your Expectations of What Graduate School Will Do for You with What It Has Done for Alumni of the Program You're Considering?

Most colleges and universities perform some kind of postgraduate survey of their students to ascertain where they are employed, what additional education they have received, and what levels of salary they are enjoying. Ask to see this information either from the university you are considering applying to or from your own alma mater, especially if it has a similar graduate program. Such surveys often reveal surprises about occupational decisions, salaries, and work satisfaction. This information may affect your decision.

The value of self-assessment (the process of examining and making decisions about your own hierarchy of values and goals) is especially important in this process of analyzing the desirability of possible career paths involving graduate education. Sometimes a job requiring advanced education seems to hold real promise but is disappointing in salary potential or number of opportunities available. Certainly it is better to research this information before embarking on a program of graduate studies. It may not change your mind about your decision, but by becoming better informed about your choice, you become better prepared for your future.

Have You Talked with People in Your Field to Explore What You Might Be Doing After Graduate School?

In pursuing your undergraduate degree, you will have come into contact with many individuals trained in the field you are considering. You might also have the opportunity to attend professional conferences, workshops, seminars, and job fairs where you can expand your network of contacts. Talk to them all!

Find out about their individual career paths, discuss your own plans and hopes, and get their feedback on the reality of your expectations, and heed their advice about your prospects. Each will have a unique tale to tell, and each will bring a different perspective on the current marketplace for the credentials you are seeking. Talking to enough people will make you an expert on what's out there.

Are You Excited by the Idea of Studying the Particular Field You Have in Mind?

This question may be the most important one of all. If you are going to spend several years in advanced study, perhaps engendering some debt or postponing some lifestyle decisions for an advanced degree, you simply ought to enjoy what you're doing. Examine your work in the discipline so far. Has it been fun? Have you found yourself exploring various paths of thought? Do you read in your area for fun? Do you enjoy talking about it, thinking about it, and sharing it with others? Advanced degrees often are the beginning of a lifetime's involvement with a particular subject. Choose carefully a field that will hold your interest and your enthusiasm.

It is fairly obvious by now that we think you should give some careful thought to your decision and take some action. If nothing else, do the following:

- Talk and question (remember to listen!)

- Reality-test

- Soul-search by yourself or with a person you trust

FINDING THE RIGHT PROGRAM FOR YOU: SOME CONSIDERATIONS

There are several important factors in coming to a sound decision about the right graduate program for you. You'll want to begin by locating institutions that offer appropriate programs, examining each of these programs and their requirements, undertaking the application process by obtaining catalogs and application materials, visiting campuses if possible, arranging for letters of recommendation, writing your application statement, and finally following up on your applications.

Locate Institutions with Appropriate Programs

Once you decide on a particular advanced degree, it's important to develop a list of schools offering such a degree program. Perhaps the best sources of graduate program information are Peterson's *Guides to Graduate Study*. Use these guides to build your list. In addition, you may want to consult the College Board's *Index of Majors and Graduate Degrees*, which will help you find graduate programs offering the degree you seek. It is indexed by academic major and then categorized by state.

Now, this may be a considerable list. You may want to narrow the choices down further by a number of criteria: tuition, availability of financial aid, public versus private institutions, U.S. versus international institutions, size of student body, size of faculty, application fee (this varies by school; most fall within the $10 to $75 range), and geographic location. This is only a partial list; you will have your own important considerations. Perhaps you are an avid scuba diver and you find it unrealistic to think you could pursue graduate study for a number of years without being able to ocean dive from time to time. Good! That's a decision and it's honest. Now, how far from the ocean is too far, and what schools meet your other needs? In any case, and according to your own criteria, begin to build a reasonable list of graduate schools that you are willing to spend the time investigating.

Examine the Degree Programs and Their Requirements

Once you've determined the criteria by which you want to develop a list of graduate schools, you can begin to examine the degree program requirements, faculty composition, and institutional research orientation. Again, using resources such as Peterson's *Guides to Graduate Study* can reveal an amazingly rich level of material by which to judge your possible selections.

In addition to degree programs and degree requirements, entries will include information about application fees, entrance test requirements, tuition, percentage of applicants accepted, numbers of applicants receiving financial aid, gender breakdown of students, numbers of full- and part-time faculty, and often gender breakdown of faculty as well. Numbers graduating in each program and research orientations of departments are also included in some entries. There is information on graduate housing, student services, and library, research, and computer facilities. A contact person, phone number, and address are also standard pieces of information in these listings. In addition to the standard entries, some schools pay an additional fee to place full-page, more detailed program descriptions. The location of such a display ad, if present, would be indicated at the end of the standard entry.

It can be helpful to draw up a chart and enter relevant information about each school you are considering in order to have a ready reference on points of information that are important to you.

Undertake the Application Process

The Catalog. Once you've decided on a selection of schools, send for catalogs and applications. It is important to note here that these materials might take many weeks to arrive. Consequently, if you need the materials quickly, it might be best to telephone and explain your situation to see whether the process can be speeded up for you. Also, check a local college or university library, which might have current and complete college catalogs in a microfiche collection. These microfiche copies can provide you with helpful information while you wait for your own copy of the graduate school catalog or bulletin to arrive.

When you receive your catalogs, give them a careful reading and make notes of issues you might want to discuss on the telephone or in a personal interview, if that's possible. Does the course selection have the depth you had hoped for?

What is the ratio of faculty to the required number of courses for your degree? How often will you encounter the same faculty member as an instructor?

....

If you are interested in graduate work in chemistry or a related field, in addition to classroom courses, consider the availability of colloquiums, directed research, specialized seminars, and other opportunities.

....

If, for example, your program offers a practicum or off-campus experience, who arranges this? Does the graduate school select a site and place you there, or is it your responsibility? What are the professional affiliations of the faculty? Does the program merit any outside professional endorsement or accreditation?

Critically evaluate the catalogs of each of the programs you are considering. List any questions you have and ask current or former teachers and colleagues for their impressions as well.

The Application. Preview each application thoroughly to determine what you need to provide in the way of letters of recommendation, transcripts from undergraduate schools or any previous graduate work, and personal essays that may be required. Make a notation for each application of what you need to complete that document.

Additionally, you'll want to determine entrance testing requirements for each institution and immediately arrange to complete your test registration. For example, the Graduate Record Exam (GRE) and most professional-school admissions tests have several weeks between the last registration date and the test date. Your local college career office should be able to provide you with test registration booklets, sample test materials, information on test sites and dates, and independent test review materials that might be available commercially.

Visit the Campus if Possible

If time and finances allow, a visit, interview, and tour can help make your decision easier. You can develop a sense of the student body, meet some of the faculty, and hear up-to-date information on resources and the curriculum. You will have a brief opportunity to "try out" the surroundings to see if they fit your needs. After all, it will be home for a while. If a visit is not possible but you have questions, don't hesitate to call and speak with the dean of the graduate school. Most are more than happy to talk to candidates and want them to have the answers they seek. Graduate school admission is a very personal and individual process.

Arrange for Letters of Recommendation

This is also the time to begin to assemble a group of individuals who will support your candidacy as a graduate student by writing letters of recommendation or completing recommendation forms. Some schools will ask you to provide letters of recommendation to be included with your application or sent directly to the school by the recommender. Other graduate programs will provide a recommendation form that must be completed by the recommender. These graduate school forms vary greatly in the amount of space provided for a written recommendation. So that you can use letters as you need to, ask your recommenders to address their letters "To Whom It May Concern," unless one of your recommenders has a particular connection to one of your graduate schools or knows an official at the school.

Choose recommenders who can speak authoritatively about the criteria important to selection officials at your graduate school. In other words, choose recommenders who can write about your grasp of the literature in your field of study, your ability to write and speak effectively, your class performance, and your demonstrated interest in the field outside of class. Other characteristics that graduate schools are interested in assessing include your emotional maturity, leadership ability, breadth of general knowledge, intellectual ability, motivation, perseverance, and ability to engage in independent inquiry.

When requesting recommendations, it's especially helpful to put the request in writing. Explain your graduate school intentions and express some of your thoughts about graduate school and your appreciation for their support. Don't be shy about "prompting" your recommenders with some suggestions of what you would appreciate being included in their comments. Most recommenders will find this direction helpful and will want to produce a statement of support that you can both stand behind. Consequently, if your interaction with one recommender was especially focused on research projects, he or she might be best able to speak of those skills and your critical thinking ability. Another recommender may have good comments to make about your public presentation skills.

Give your recommenders plenty of lead time in which to complete your recommendation, and set a date by which they should respond. If they fail to meet your deadline, be prepared to make a polite call or visit to inquire if they need more information or if there is anything you can do to move the process along.

Whether or not you are providing a graduate school form or asking for an original letter to be mailed, be sure to provide an envelope and postage if the recommender must mail the form or letter directly to the graduate school.

Each recommendation you request should provide a different piece of information about you for the selection committee. It might be pleasant for letters of recommendation to say that you are a fine, upstanding individual, but a selection committee for graduate school will require specific information. Each recommender has had a unique relationship with you, and their letters should reflect that. Think of each letter as helping to build a more complete portrait of you as a potential graduate student.

Write Your Application Statement

· ·

For the chemistry major interested in graduate study, the application should be a welcome opportunity to express your deep interest in pursuing further study. Your understanding of the challenges ahead, your commitment to the work involved, and your expressed self-awareness will weigh along with grades and test scores in the decision process of the graduate school admissions committee.

· ·

An excellent source to help in thinking about writing this essay is *How to Write a Winning Personal Statement for Graduate and Professional School* by Richard J. Stelzer. It has been written from the perspective of what graduate school selection committees are looking for when they read these essays. It provides helpful tips to keep your essay targeted on the kinds of issues and criteria that are important to selection committees and that provide them with the kind of information they can best utilize in making their decision.

Follow Up on Your Applications

After you have finished each application and mailed it along with your transcript requests and letters of recommendation, be sure to follow up on the progress of your file. For example, call the graduate school administrative staff to see whether your transcripts have arrived. If the school required your recommenders to fill out a specific recommendation form that had to be mailed directly to the school, you will want to ensure that they have all arrived in good time for the processing of your application. It is your responsibility to make certain that all required information is received by the institution.

RESEARCHING FINANCIAL AID SOURCES, SCHOLARSHIPS, AND FELLOWSHIPS

Financial aid information is available from each school, so be sure to request it when you call for a catalog and application materials. There will be several lengthy forms to complete, and these will vary by school, type of school (public versus private), and state. Be sure to note the deadline dates for these important forms.

There are many excellent resources available to help you explore all of your financial aid options. Visit your college career office or local public library to find out about the range of materials available. Two excellent resources include Peterson's *Grants for Graduate Students* and the Foundation Center's *Foundation Grants to Individuals.* These types of resources generally contain information that can be accessed by indexes including field of study, specific eligibility requirements, administering agency, and geographic focus.

EVALUATING ACCEPTANCES

If you apply to and are accepted at more than one school, it is time to return to your initial research and self-assessment to evaluate your options and select the program that will best help you achieve the goals you set for pursuing graduate study. You'll want to choose a program that will allow you to complete your studies in a timely and cost-effective way. This may be a good time to get additional feedback from professors and career professionals who are familiar with your interests and plans. Ultimately, the decision is yours, so be sure you get answers to all the questions you can think of.

SOME NOTES ABOUT REJECTION

Each graduate school is searching for applicants who appear to have the qualifications necessary to succeed in its program. Applications are evaluated on a combination of undergraduate grade point average, strength of letters of recommendation, standardized test scores, and personal statements written for the application.

A carelessly completed application is one reason some applicants are denied admission to a graduate program. To avoid this type of needless rejection, be sure to carefully and completely answer all appropriate questions on the application form, focus your personal statement given the instructions provided, and submit your materials well in advance of the deadline. Remember that your test scores and recommendations are considered a part of your application, so they must also be received by the deadline.

If you are rejected by a school that especially interests you, you may want to contact the dean of graduate studies to discuss the strengths and weaknesses of your application. Information provided by the dean will be useful in reapplying to the program or applying to other, similar programs.

PART TWO

THE CAREER PATHS

CHAPTER NINE

INTRODUCTION TO THE CHEMISTRY CAREER PATHS

*C*hemistry is a complex field. It involves both theoretical and practical aspects. Most people probably regard chemists as highly intelligent types, and that is understandable, for a true grasp of chemistry requires some rather deep thinking. Do you have a flair for math? Are you able to grasp abstract concepts? These traits, along with the capacity for problem-solving, are common in those who are successful in the field.

At the same time, everyone who pursues a career related to chemistry doesn't do the same kind of work. So there is room for people with a wide range of interests and abilities.

AREAS OF STUDY IN CHEMISTRY

In its most basic terms, chemistry consists of the study of matter. This includes the way matter is composed and how elements combine to form compounds, among other topics. Within this field, students and researchers tend to focus their attention on a variety of areas. Following is a description of some of the primary areas of study within the overall field of chemistry.

General Chemistry

A chemist who doesn't specialize in any particular field (such as a high school teacher) might deal with any of the basic fundamentals of chemistry. This can include atomic structure, chemical bonding, states of matter, and the nature of solutions. Other topics might include chemical kinetics, equilibrium, the laws of thermodynamics, nuclear chemistry, electrochemistry, and organic chemistry.

Analytical Chemistry

This area of chemistry deals with chemical analysis though a variety of methods, including both qualitative and quantitative chemical analysis. The use of different types of instrumentation is a major focus. Analytical chemists use techniques such as absorption and emission spectroscopy, potentiometry, and gas chromatography to complete their work.

Organic Chemistry

Organic chemists study the structure and properties of hydrocarbons. They may focus on the chemistry of halides, alcohols, phenols, carbohydrates, proteins, or other compounds. How do organic compounds behave? How do they occur in nature? How can they be used in industrial applications or for other purposes? These are some of the questions addressed by organic chemists.

Inorganic Chemistry

Inorganic chemistry covers a great deal of territory, and of course can be broken up into numerous smaller fields of study. It includes atomic structure and the principles of chemical bonding, acids and bases, and many of the basic concepts of chemical interaction. Learning and working with inorganic chemistry may range from your first study of the elements of the periodic table to the synthesis of inorganic compounds.

Biochemistry

This area deals with the chemistry of living organisms. Biochemists may work with cellular metabolism, protein synthesis, or other processes. With the exciting developments being made in the life sciences, this field of study is a rapidly changing one.

Physical Chemistry

Physical chemistry covers basic laws and theories of chemistry such as thermodynamics, quantum mechanics, and kinetics. This can include quantum theory, the applications of thermodynamics to chemical systems, electrochemistry, and other areas of scientific theory and practice.

Geochemistry

Geochemists apply their understanding of chemistry to the earth and environmental sciences. They deal with topics such as the evolution of rocks, mineral stability, water chemistry, and geochemical cycles.

Polymer Chemistry

This area of chemistry deals with the nature and structure of polymers. A typical application of polymer chemistry might be the synthesis of materials for industrial or commercial applications.

Other Areas of Study

Other areas of study range from specialized areas such as superconductivity or adhesives research, to applications such as the chemical analyses used in criminal forensics.

ADVANTAGE OF A DEGREE

Earning a college degree is certainly a worthwhile accomplishment. But in today's competitive world, a bachelor's degree is not always a quick ticket to a great job. With more people attending college than ever before, a degree is not as special as it once was. And the shifting nature of an evolving economy has brought much uncertainty when it comes to careers.

This is especially true in chemistry and other scientific fields, where a higher proportion of workers hold advanced degrees than in most other career areas. This means that the holder of a bachelor's degree may be at a disadvantage when compared with those who have earned a doctoral or master's degree.

Nevertheless, a bachelor's degree is almost always an asset. Sooner or later, most people who earn a college degree find that it substantially advances their career choices. Certainly, a college degree holds value for its own sake. But a degree can also be a major factor in landing a good job. Even though higher education has become more accessible than ever, only about 20 percent of American adults hold a bachelor's degree or higher, according to the U.S. Census. Put another way, this means that four out of five adults in the United States lack a college degree. When you're seeking employment or attempting to advance on the job, a degree can make the difference.

For research or teaching jobs requiring an advanced degree, a bachelor's degree still holds great value as a first degree. It starts you on the way to further education and is a necessary prerequisite to earning a master's or doctoral degree.

Chemistry graduates not only benefit from the specialized knowledge needed to pursue a career in the sciences, but also from the general studies or liberal arts components of a bachelor's degree program. The combination of general and specific knowledge prepares chemistry graduates to perform a wide range of tasks in their careers and personal lives.

TYPICAL CAREER PATHS

In its brochure "Chemistry and Your Career," the American Chemical Society (ACS) points out there is no single, typical career path for a chemistry major. According to the ACS, a breakout of employers of chemists is as follows:

❑ Nearly 50 percent of chemists work in research

❑ Approximately 60 percent of chemists are employed in the chemical industry

❑ About one-fourth (24 percent) of chemists work in schools, colleges, or other academic institutions

❑ About 9 percent of chemists are employed by government agencies

In addition to the major areas of employment, some chemists work in a variety of what may be considered nontraditional career areas. These include writers, patent lawyers, technical librarians, and specialists in conserving works of art.

A look at the career paths followed by graduates of any college or university where chemistry is taught can be revealing. For example, Salve Regina University in Newport, Rhode Island recently profiled some of the graduates of its chemistry program and the types of jobs they are now doing.

In the area of research and development, chemistry grads are applying scientific knowledge for purposes such as developing new or improved substances and understanding and controlling the behavior of materials. Their job titles and employers include:

Application chemist, Loctite Corporation

Chemist, Océ—Imaging Supplies

Chemist, Sureguard, Inc.

Chemist/engineer, Raytheon Electronics Systems

Process development chemist, Pfizer, Inc.

Research assistant, Roger Williams Hospital

Research associate, Biopure

Senior associate scientist, Warner-Lambert

Staff scientist, EIC Labs

Teaching and research assistant, University of California, San Diego

Teaching and research assistant, University of Massachusetts

In the area of biotechnology, where many techniques have been adapted from chemistry, one graduate is working as a lab technician at Rhode Island Hospital.

In forensic science, where state and federal law enforcement organizations use chemists in forensic laboratories, an alumnus is working as a forensic chemist for the Bureau of Alcohol, Tobacco, and Firearms.

Environmental chemistry is another area in which alumni are employed. Salve Regina faculty point out that career possibilities in this area include work in environment analysis firms, in industry dealing with emission control and abatement, and in state and federal government testing and regulatory agencies.

Other graduates have found that a bachelor's degree in chemistry is a suitable program for entrance to medical school or to study dentistry or veterinary medicine. Some with advanced degrees work in biomedical or pharmacological research. Others work as pharmacists. Other jobs held by chemistry graduates include:

Buyer	Manager, fine chemical department
Compliance manager	Materials engineer
Consultant	Pharmaceutical sales representative
Director, sales and marketing	Quality control specialist
Guidance counselor	Teacher
Lab manager	Technical writer

Other colleges and universities can cite similar examples. The exciting message for chemistry majors is that there is not just a single career direction to follow. The sky may not be the limit, but it's close!

Many students who earn a bachelor's degree in chemistry go on to pursue a master's degree or a doctorate or professional degree. This is a frequent choice of chemistry majors who hope to enhance their careers. Most commonly, the graduate degree will also be in chemistry or in a closely related or more specialized field, such as biochemistry. Or it might be in a completely different field such as education, business administration, law, engineering, or medicine.

Whether they go to graduate school or enter the workforce after completing a bachelor's degree, chemistry majors end up working in a wide range of career areas. As with most undergraduate fields, studying chemistry also involves exposure to other liberal arts fields. This in turn builds a firm foundation for functioning in the modern world and for thinking critically. The tools learned in college, from reading and writing with skill to analyzing and understanding complex information, prepare students to adapt to a variety of workplace needs. From the research chemist who develops new processes to the high school teacher who introduces students to the scientific method, those who choose to master chemistry find it can be the basis for an exciting and productive career.

The following chapters cover some of the career paths that can be followed in this field. They are not exhaustive, but they should provide a good overview of some of the possibilities that await you. These career paths are:

1. Research and development

2. Teaching

3. Chemical engineering

4. Science management and support

These major career paths are offered as realistic suggestions, with the objective of stimulating your thinking about possible career directions. You will also be able to think of other possible career paths. In any case, you should be able to make a case for your bachelor's degree in chemistry in a wide range of job situations.

CHAPTER TEN

PATH 1: RESEARCH AND DEVELOPMENT

A s a chemistry major, you understand the importance of chemistry and the other physical sciences. You realize that the work of chemists touches all of our lives many times every day. From the plastics making up kitchen utensils to the gasoline powering your car, the benefits of chemistry can be found in virtually every aspect of modern life. None of these advances would have been possible without the initial research and subsequent development efforts of chemists.

DEFINITION OF THE CAREER PATH

"Research and development" is a broad term. To begin to define this term within the context of career planning, here are some basic facts about research chemistry and related areas as a career path.

- Chemical research takes place in a variety of formats and at different levels. It can mean working in a small lab or as part of a large team at a multinational corporation.

- Research positions include jobs at various levels, from low-level research assistants to those managing other chemists and support personnel.

- Some research jobs involve working for noncommercial, nonprofit organizations. Others involve conducting research and development for companies whose main goal is to earn profits.

POSSIBLE JOB TITLES

The U.S. Department of Labor lists a wide range of job titles in its *Dictionary of Occupational Titles.* Among those classified under "chemist" are:

Analytical chemist	Lab technician
Assayer	Laboratory tester
Biochemist	Organic chemist
Chemical laboratory chief	Perfumer
Chemical laboratory technician	Pharmaceutical chemist
Chief chemist	Physical chemist
Clinical chemist	Proteins chemist
Colorist	Steroids chemist
Director, chemical laboratory	Toxicologist
Director of research	Wastewater treatment plant chemist
Food chemist	Water purification chemist
Inorganic chemist	Yeast culture developer
Instrumentation chemist	

In addition, employers use titles such as:

Application chemist	Research chemist
Assistant chief chemist	Senior associate scientist
Chemist/engineer	Senior scientist
Process development chemist	Staff scientist
Research associate	

REPRESENTATIVE RESEARCH AND DEVELOPMENT JOBS

Jobs in research and development cover a wide range of duties for a variety of employers. Chemists involved in basic research investigate the properties, composition, and structure of matter. They also look at the laws governing the combination of elements and reactions of substances.

Chemists who work in applied research and development apply their knowledge to practical problems and needs. Often this means creating new products or improving existing ones. For example, a chemist might work to make an adhesive compound more useful for industrial applications.

Many chemists work in production and inspection in manufacturing plants. They prepare instructions for plant workers for mixing and processing chemicals, monitor automated processes, test results of chemical reactions, complete reports, and perform other tasks.

GOVERNMENT RESEARCH AND DEVELOPMENT

Chemists who work for government agencies tackle problems of interest to that particular agency or branch of government. For example, at the Human Exposure and Atmospheric Sciences Division of the National Exposure Research Laboratory, chemists develop immunochemical and instrumental methods to support environmental monitoring and human exposure assessment studies. Specific duties include:

❑ Performing simple organic synthesis such as protein and hapten conjugation for development of immunologic reagents

❑ Performing method evaluation studies to assess the suitability of individual methods for environmental monitoring and human exposure assessment studies

❑ Performing analytical field work, such as pilot monitoring studies

❑ Preparing progress and summary reports for use in EPA reports and for peer-reviewed manuscripts

❑ Participating in the design and conduct of targeted field studies to advance the human exposure database

❑ Documenting the results of research

❑ Presenting the results of research at scientific meetings or conferences

At the Centers for Disease Control and Prevention National Center for Infectious Diseases, chemists perform a variety of functions. For one typical position, this might include the following duties:

❑ Developing methods for and serving as a technical authority for the branch's major chemical instrumentation, including time-of-flight mass spectrometer, surface-plasmon resonance biosensor, spectrofluometer, UV/visible and diode-array spectrometers, and capillary chromatographic and electrophoretic apparatus

❑ Serving as technical authority relative to protein chemistry electrorobotic processes

❑ Manipulating, interpreting, and preparing publishable images of the data generated by instrumentation

❑ Overseeing the instrumentational and computational aspects of the section's functions and serving as a resource person to scientists working with DNA chemistry and molecular biology

At the Food and Drug Administration (FDA), chemists review and evaluate New Drug Applications (NDAs). In this capacity, they deal with chemical components and evaluation of adequacy of the methods, facilities, and controls used for the manufacture of drugs. FDA chemists review proposed labels, summarize findings, and make recommendations for approval or nonapproval of applications. They might also conduct research projects, such as studying the effects of food components and dietary supplements or investigating the effects of drugs, antibiotics, and agricultural chemicals on cattle, small laboratory animals, and other domestic livestock. FDA chemists work in the Office of the Commissioner, Office of Regulatory Affairs, Center for Biologics Evaluation and Research, Center for Drug Evaluation and Research, Center for Veterinary Medicine, Center for Devices and Radiological Health, and the Center for Food Safety and Applied Nutrition.

Industrial Research and Development

A major area of employment for chemists is the sprawling chemical industry, which constitutes one of the world's major areas of industrial development. Ranging from small firms specializing in a single product to huge corporations, these companies employ thousands of chemists.

For example, National Starch and Chemical Company employs chemists in research, product development, process development, manufacturing, and technical services. Chemists join engineers, systems analysts, and other professionals in refining existing products and developing new ones. This includes work with foods, paper, and other products. Chemists work at the company's world headquarters in Bridgewater, New Jersey, and at its major manufacturing plants in Indiana, Illinois, North Carolina, South Carolina, and Missouri.

Chemists employed by Eastman Kodak Company, headquartered in Rochester, New York, support that company's efforts in developing photographic products and processes. They work in areas such as photographic imaging, digital imaging, and electronic products.

Hundreds of other companies employ chemists in positions ranging from entry-level chemists or technicians to senior-level scientists. Major corporations such as DuPont, Dow, Procter & Gamble, and Rohm and Haas, as well as smaller entrepreneurial firms, employ chemists to conduct research and development activities. Their duties vary, but may include such tasks as:

❑ Developing new and improved products such as adhesives, drugs, cosmetics, synthetic fibers, paints, lubricants, and electronic components

❑ Developing processes that save energy and reduce pollution in areas such as oil refining and petrochemical processing

❑ Conducting and overseeing production processes in various areas of chemical manufacturing

❑ Providing quality control functions

❑ Monitoring automated production processes

❑ Testing samples of raw materials, products in production, or finished products

❑ Developing or improving testing methods

If you want to follow a career path that is most directly related to your studies as a chemistry major, then working in research and development is a logical step. Whether this means employment in private industry or with a government agency or other organization, research and development careers hold great potential for the motivated chemistry major.

Other Research and Development

Some chemists work neither for government agencies nor private companies. Universities, for example, also employ chemists (see Chapter 12 on teaching). Some who work for educational institutions, however, do little or no teaching, but instead conduct research. Some other chemists are self-employed, occasionally operating their own research and development businesses.

POSSIBLE EMPLOYERS

As we've noted, research and development jobs can be found in a wide range of agencies and organizations. Some jobs involve employment with universities or colleges. Others consist of working for federal or state government agencies. The private sector is a major area of employment, from large chemical or petroleum companies to small specialty firms.

Here are some possible employers of chemists and related personnel:

Agricultural products companies

Beverage manufacturers

Biotechnology firms

Broad-based chemical manufacturers

Centers for Disease Control and Prevention

Electronics companies

Environmental engineering firms

Food and Drug Administration

Food manufacturers

National Aeronautics and Space Administration

National Institutes of Health

Nuclear Regulatory Commission

Oil and gas companies

Paint manufacturers

Pharmaceutical manufacturers

Plastics manufacturers

Pulp and paper companies

Rubber processing firms

Soap and detergent manufacturers

Specialty chemical companies

State environmental management agencies

Textile companies

Universities and colleges

U.S. Department of Agriculture

U.S. Department of Defense

U.S. Department of Health and Human Services

U.S. Environmental Protection Agency

Waste treatment facilities

WORKING CONDITIONS

Because research jobs range from academic settings to those in industrial environments, working conditions vary widely. In general, workers in this field enjoy comfortable working conditions.

Typically, research jobs involve a significant amount of laboratory work as well as time spent in office settings. Laboratory settings range from small, simply equipped labs to large, well-equipped facilities. Some are well lit and virtually spotless; others have more of an industrial or production character. Some researchers also conduct work in outdoor settings as a part of plant operations or industrial-scale experiments.

Office settings may vary from a tiny, single cubicle to an expansive office with plush furnishings. Often the latter is an indicator of authority and seniority, with senior researchers enjoying offices that are larger and more impressive than those of junior personnel. But this is by no means a standard practice.

Both office and laboratory environments may vary depending on a number of factors: the size and age of the building in which research facilities are located; the way in which office space has historically been apportioned within an organization; staffing trends resulting in increases or reductions in the demand for lab or office space; and other considerations.

A major element within the laboratory environment is equipment. Items ranging from glassware to testing equipment make up a significant part of any lab setting. In addition, the presence of chemicals themselves affects the working environment. In some cases, annoying smells or irritating vapors may be present. Some chemicals are quite dangerous, causing the need for extreme caution. Safety equipment such as gloves, goggles, fume hoods, and other items is common.

Research chemists also work at desks and within offices, where they complete lab reports, read journal articles, and operate computers. Regardless of the size or furnishings of an office, it typically includes a few basics such as a desk, chair, telephone, and computer. Related work environments may include conference rooms, offices of co-workers, and large meeting rooms.

TRAINING AND QUALIFICATIONS

For research jobs, a bachelor's degree or higher is required for all but technician-level positions. In the academic community, a doctorate is often expected. In private industry, a Ph.D. may also be required, but some jobs can be found with a bachelor's or master's degree. Because the doctorate is rather common within the scientific community, though, it is important to realize that even when an advanced degree is not strictly required, the applicant pool for any given position may include applicants with advanced educational preparation. In some cases, only a bachelor's is required, but having an advanced degree can make you more competitive.

For jobs with the federal government, a bachelor's degree may be sufficient to qualify for many positions. If you hold a bachelor's degree, you're eligible for appointment at the GS-5 level (see section on earnings for a description of this system for classifying government jobs, page 125).

One direction to go after completing a bachelor's degree with a major in chemistry is to pursue a medical degree and then conduct medical research. Another possibility is to complete an advanced degree in a different or related field. For example, a bachelor's in chemistry might be followed by a master's in biology, mathematics, computer science, or some other field.

More typically, students complete an advanced degree in chemistry. This may come immediately after finishing a bachelor's degree, or after having gained some work experience.

Graduate course offerings in chemistry cover many of the same areas as those offered at the undergraduate level, but in greater depth and with increasing levels of specialization.

For example, the Department of Chemistry at the University of Kentucky offers the following advanced or graduate-level courses:

Advanced Analytical Chemistry

Advanced Inorganic Chemistry

Advanced Quantum Chemistry

Chemical Instrumentation

Chemical Kinetics

Chemical Separations

Chemical Thermodynamics

Chemistry of the Transition Metals

Communication in Chemistry

Descriptive Inorganic Chemistry

Dissertation Research

Electrochemical Methods of Analysis

Graduate Seminar

Individual Work in Chemistry

Instrumental Analysis

Master's Thesis Research

Membrane Sciences Colloquium

Nuclear Chemistry

Optical Methods of Analysis

Organotransition Metal Chemistry

Physical Organic Chemistry

Practicum in Chemistry Instruction

Principles of Organic Chemistry

Principles of Physical Chemistry I (Quantum Chemistry)

Principles of Physical Chemistry II

Qualitative Organic Analysis Laboratory

Radiochemistry

Radiochemistry Laboratory

Research in Chemistry

Residence Credit for Doctor's Degree

Residence Credit for Master's Degree

Short Topics in Chemistry

Spectrometric Identification of Organic Compounds

Spectroscopy and Photophysics

Synthetic Organic Chemistry

Topics in Chemistry

Topics in Inorganic Chemistry

Topics in Organic Chemistry

At George Washington University in Washington, D.C., the master's degree program in chemistry offers two options for students who have completed a bachelor's degree with a major in chemistry.

Under the thesis option, students complete thirty credit hours of approved courses, including a thesis research course that may be in analytical, inorganic, organic, or physical chemistry.

Under the no-thesis option, thirty-six credit hours of approved courses are required. This may include up to nine credit hours in other departments relevant to the student's area of interest.

With both options, students must meet the university's general requirements, demonstrate proficiency in computer programming, and pass a master's comprehensive examination.

In addition, the university offers a master of science in geochemistry, a five-year bachelor of science/master of science in chemical toxicology, and a doctor of philosophy in chemistry. Within the Ph.D. program, research fields include analytical and molecular spectroscopy; catalysis; chemical instrumentation; combustion chemistry; electrochemistry; environmental chemistry; forensic chemistry; inorganic and organometallics synthesis; organic synthesis/natural products; structure and reactivity studies; surface, interface, and materials science; theoretical chemistry; trace and polymer analysis; and transition metal complexes.

Other universities offer similar graduate programs. In addition, some offer highly specialized degree options. To find out more, check any school's catalog. Also, more and more colleges and universities are now operating Web sites that you can easily access via the Internet.

EARNINGS

Those employed in research jobs earn a wide range of salaries. On the average, experienced chemists earn more than $50,000 per year.

According to a survey by the American Chemical Society, ACS members reported the following median salaries earned in 1997:

EDUCATIONAL LEVEL	MEDIAN SALARY
Bachelor's degree	$49,400
Master's degree	$56,200
Ph.D.	$71,000

On average, chemists working in private industry earn the highest salaries, and of course experienced workers earn higher salaries than beginning ones. Recent graduates with a bachelor's degree are more likely to earn $25,000 to $35,000 yearly than the figures cited above. Those with some work experience or who have completed internships tend to command higher starting salaries than those who have not yet worked in the field.

Chemists who work for the federal government or for state governments tend to earn salaries that are somewhat lower than those in private industry. But at the same time, as government employees they enjoy excellent job security as well as good benefits.

For personnel employed by the federal government, salaries may be established by a highly structured plan known as the General Schedule (GS) plan. Under this system, jobs are rated at fifteen different levels based on a combination of job demands and qualifications needed to fill the position. Specific salaries are attached to each level.

For 1998, basic pay under the GS plan was as follows:

GS-1 $12,960	GS-6 $22,258	GS-11 $36,609
GS-2 $14,571	GS-7 $22,734	GS-12 $43,876
GS-3 $15,899	GS-8 $27,393	GS-13 $52,176
GS-4 $17,848	GS-9 $30,257	GS-14 $61,656
GS-5 $19,969	GS-10 $33,320	GS-15 $72,525

These figures represent base salaries, but most jobs actually pay more. The government adjusts GS pay geographically, and when locality payments are included, pay rates within the continental United States may go as much as 12 percent higher. Outside the continental United States, pay rates are 10 to 25 percent higher.

In addition, some starting salaries are higher in hard-to-fill fields. And experienced employees tend to build up higher salaries as time on the job lengthens.

What if you have a college degree in chemistry science but no directly related job experience? According to the U.S. Office of Personnel Management, you would start out at a GS-5 level. If you maintained a B average or meet other academic credentials, you can start at GS-7. If you have a master's degree directly related to the job in question, you can qualify for a GS-9 rating.

At the state and local level, salaries vary tremendously from one state to the next or among different branches of government and different departments. To get an idea of salaries for jobs in your city or state, check ads for job openings, or consult officials at government agencies in which you are interested.

IDENTIFYING JOB OPENINGS

You can follow a number of strategies to identify job openings. Here are just some of them.

- Take advantage of your college or university placement office

- Attend career fairs or job fairs

- Participate in internships and use them to make contacts

- Consult classified ads in newspapers and professional publications

- Sign up with job-placement firms

- Obtain information about potential employers through Internet resources

- Participate in professional organizations and use any job search services they provide

The U.S. government's Office of Personnel Management lists job openings on a continuous basis. This includes posting such openings on its Internet Web site (www.opm.gov). For any given week, hundreds of job openings with the federal government are listed.

Another source of information about government jobs is "Jobs in Government." This is a free online service that identifies government job openings. For information, write to:

Jobs in Government
P.O. Box 1436
Agoura Hills, CA 91376

Or, go to their Web site at www.jobsingovernment.com.

For Canadians, a good source of job ads that include public service positions is:

Canadian Employment Weekly
15 Madison Avenue
Toronto, Ontario
Canada M5R 2S2

Each weekly issue of this publication lists more than 500 new position openings, including jobs in every province and territory of Canada.

JOINING PROFESSIONAL ORGANIZATIONS

Perhaps while you're still a chemistry major, and certainly later as a professional in the field, you will want to join one or more professional organizations (see the list of representative organizations at the end of this chapter, page 131). The benefits of such groups can include the following:

❑ Annual meetings or other regular meetings that provide members an opportunity to interact and discuss matters of common professional interest

❑ Special-topic conferences on specific research areas or other topics of interest to members

❑ Networking activities that can help in the job search process, among other benefits

❑ Publications ranging from professional journals to newsletters, books, and other publications

❑ Forums for exchange of ideas with other members and sometimes with the public

❑ Information on the state of the profession (such as salary surveys and studies on supply and demand for chemists and related personnel)

❑ Job listings and job-referral services

❑ Member services in areas such as group insurance

❑ Clearinghouse services on matters of public interest related to the profession

The premier organization in the field is the American Chemical Society (ACS), headquartered in Washington, D.C. The ACS has more than 150,000 members. It offers an impressive array of services, including career guidance and educational programs. With more than thirty different divisions, the ACS publishes a large number of helpful publications, sponsors conferences and other meetings, conducts surveys, and performs a variety of other highly useful functions. If you plan to be a professional in the field, you need to be affiliated with the American Chemical Society. For more details, contact the ACS at:

American Chemical Society
1155 16th Street NW
Washington, D.C. 20036

A similar organization serving residents of Canada is the Canadian Society for Chemistry (CSC). It is one of three constituent societies of the Chemical Institute of Canada.

The CSC promotes the practice and application of chemistry in Canada. It represents chemistry professionals, promotes high standards of chemical education, and encourages high-quality research and development efforts. The CSC also assists decision-makers in government and elsewhere in reaching informed decisions related to chemistry. It also provides a variety of individual services for members, including scholarships and educational offerings.

One of the CSC's most important functions is accrediting chemistry programs at Canadian universities. It also sponsors student chapters at campuses across Canada and holds several regional student conferences each year. For more details, contact the CSC at:

Canadian Society for Chemistry
130 Slater Street, Suite 550
Ottawa, Ontario
Canada K1P 6E2

Other professional associations focus on the interests of specific fields or subfields. Examples include the American Association of Cereal Chemists, the American Petroleum Institute, and the Council for Chemical Research.

For details on such organizations, see the list at the end of this chapter (page 131).

Benefits of Membership

Although membership requirements vary, most organizations in chemistry or related fields require that potential members meet at least one of the following to qualify for full membership:

1. Hold a bachelor's degree or advanced degree in chemistry, chemical engineering, or a closely related field

2. Hold special credentials as approved by a membership committee

3. Be a graduate student in chemistry, chemical engineering, or a related field, or hold a postgraduate research position

In addition, undergraduate students often qualify for special student-member status.

TRY AN INTERNSHIP

If you want to gain valuable experience while still a student, consider serving as an intern. Internships in government labs, industrial laboratories, or other organizations can provide valuable opportunities to supplement learning that takes place in the classroom.

When you serve as an intern, you gain an inside look at what it's like to work in research and development. You also make contacts that can prove valuable in the future for job references and other purposes. In some cases, internships can lead directly to future employment with the agency you serve.

Some students serve as interns while still completing an undergraduate degree. Others seek internships as a part of master's or doctoral programs.

An interesting opportunity of this type is the Image Science Career Development Program offered by Eastman Kodak Company. It consists of a two-year career development program within Kodak's research and development area. The program provides each participant with a mentor and a study curriculum in image science. In addition, participants benefit from a formalized job rotation program that exposes them to different departments and research areas.

The main purpose of the program is preparing people to take technical leadership roles in research and product development programs. Persons with a bachelor's degree in chemical engineering are eligible to apply, along with graduates in other sciences such as computer science, physics, and software engineering. For more information, write to:

Image Science Career Development Program
Eastman Kodak Company
1700 Dewey Avenue
Kodak Research Laboratory
Rochester, NY 14650-01908

REPRESENTATIVE INTERNSHIP SPONSORS

Representative sponsors of internships include:

Ames Laboratory

Argonne National Laboratories

Brookhaven National Laboratory

Ernest Orlando Lawrence Berkeley
National Laboratory

Fermi National Accelerator
Laboratory

Major chemical companies

National Institute for Standards
and Technology

National Institutes of Health

National Renewable Energy
Laboratory

National Science Foundation

Oak Ridge National Laboratories

Pittsburgh Energy and Technology
Center

Princeton Plasma Physics Laboratory

Stanford Linear Accelerator Center

University-based research projects

U.S. Department of Energy

Typical duties for interns include:

- Conducting lab research
- Assisting senior scientists in developing new processes
- Completing written reports of research
- Working with new or innovative equipment
- Assisting in researching and designing project methodologies
- Duplicating or replicating experimental results

STRATEGY FOR FINDING JOBS

In seeking a job in your field, consider these steps:

1. Consult professors and college placement counselors to obtain information about job opportunities and especially advice about how your own skills and achievements can best be used.

2. Contact government agencies, corporations, newspapers, and professional associations to find out about other job opportunities.

3. Prepare a resume that highlights your chemistry background, analytical and communication skills, internship and job experiences, and knowledge you've gained from chemistry courses.

4. Send your resume to employers that interest you, and consult your placement office to schedule interviews with employers who will be visiting your campus.

5. Talk with people working in organizations that interest you and seek suggestions regarding possible employment.

6. Pursue an internship while still in college with an organization you find interesting.

Remember, it's never too early to begin taking concrete steps that will support your job search. Keep in close touch with professors, counselors, and placement office staff, and maintain records that will help you in seeking employment.

RELATED OCCUPATIONS

The skills that chemistry majors bring to jobs in research and development are also valued in a number of related occupations. Here is a small sample of job areas that draw on similar skills to some degree.

Agricultural scientist

Biologist

Chemical engineer

Chemical technician

Chemistry teacher

Physician

Physicist

Professor

Research manager

Science writer

PROFESSIONAL ASSOCIATIONS FOR RESEARCH AND DEVELOPMENT CHEMISTS

American Association of Cereal Chemists
3340 Pilot Knob Road
St. Paul, MN 55121
Members/Purpose: Supports interests of professionals studying the chemistry of cereal grains and its products and those working in related fields.
Training: Annual meeting and short courses.
Journals/Publications: *Cereal Chemistry*, *Cereal Foods World*, books on cereal and food science.
Job Listings: Offers placement service.

American Chemical Society
1155 16th Street NW
Washington, D.C. 20036
Members/Purpose: Serves more than 150,000 members as a broad-based society for chemists and chemical engineers.
Training: Provides courses, seminars, and workshops.
Journals/Publications: *Journal of the American Chemical Society*; *Chemical and Engineering News*; *ChemTech*; many other publications.
Job Listings: Offers career guidance counseling.

American Institute of Chemical Engineers
United Engineering Center
345 East 47th Street
New York, NY 10017

Members/Purpose: Fifty-eight thousand chemical engineers in industry, academia, and government. Members include engineers and supporters of engineering at all levels, including students, practicing engineers, and managers.

Training: Holds two major conferences each year, including an annual meeting; sponsors specialized topical conferences, meetings, and expositions. Also offers a modular instruction series for self-study.

Journals/Publications: *Chemical Engineering Progress*, a monthly magazine for CPI professionals; *AIChE Journal*, a peer-reviewed monthly journal; *Environmental Progress*; *Process Safety Progress*.

American Petroleum Institute
1220 L Street NW
Washington, D.C. 20005

Members/Purpose: Serves as a forum for all parts of the oil and natural gas industry; pursues public policy objectives; advances interests of the industry.

Journals/Publications: Various booklets and technical publications; newsletter, *API Reports*.

Education: Offers seminars, workshops, and symposia; provides training materials.

Canadian Society for Chemistry
130 Slater Street, Suite 550
Ottawa, Ontario
Canada K1P 6E2

Members/Purpose: A constituent member of the Chemical Institute of Canada (CIC). Promotes the practice and application of chemistry in Canada. Members include professional chemists, chemistry faculty, students, and others. Accredits chemistry programs at Canadian universities.

Journal/Publication: *Canadian Chemical News* (published by CIC).

Training: Holds an annual national conference; sponsors student chapters at campuses across Canada and holds several regional student conferences each year.

Council for Chemical Research
1620 L Street NW #620
Washington, D.C. 20036

Members/Purpose: Supports research in chemistry-based sciences, engineering, and technology; promotes interaction among industrial, academic, and governmental research sectors.

Journals/Publications: Publishes a directory of industrial and government laboratory speakers.

Training: Holds an annual meeting; sponsors technology seminars.

North American Catalysis Society

c/o Barbara K. Warren, Union Carbide Corporation

P.O. Box 8361

South Charleston, WV 25303

Members/Purpose: Promotes the growth and development of the science of catalysis and related scientific disciplines. Affiliated with thirteen local Catalysis Clubs and Societies in North America.

Publication: Publishes a quarterly newsletter.

Training: Holds a major meeting every two years.

Synthetic Organic Chemical Manufacturers Association

1850 M Street NW, Suite 700

Washington, D.C. 20036

Members/Purpose: Represents the legislative, regulatory, and commercial interests of more than 300 member companies, including specialty producers and large multinational corporations.

Soap and Detergent Association

475 Park Avenue South

New York, NY 10016

Members/Purpose: A national trade association representing approximately 135 manufacturers of household, industrial, and institutional cleaning products, and other related items. Members include United States, Canadian, and Mexican companies. Advances public understanding of the safety and benefits of cleaning products, and protects the ability of members to formulate products that best meet consumer needs.

Training: Sponsors seminars and conferences.

CHAPTER 11

PATH 2: TEACHING

*I*n studying chemistry, you have developed an understanding of the different elements, the ways they combine into various compounds, and some of the applications of this knowledge. But you probably would never have acquired such information if not for the work of teachers. From your first science studies in elementary school to the advanced courses you have taken as a chemistry major, teachers have been essential to your learning.

As you make plans for your own future, one option is to take on the role of teacher. If you obtain the right credentials and develop the necessary skills, your career might include the teaching of chemistry or related subjects.

DEFINITION OF THE CAREER PATH

Chemistry is a highly respected and long-standing academic discipline. It is taught widely in colleges and universities. Students who choose to major or minor in the field are an important audience, but their numbers are small compared to other students who take chemistry classes as a part of their general studies, as requirements in other fields, or as electives.

Students who major in nursing and other health fields normally take chemistry courses. Those who major in other scientific fields, such as biology, complete courses in chemistry. The same is true of a variety of other fields, ranging from forestry engineering to forensics.

At the high school level, classes in chemistry are frequently required for college-bound students. Most states and school districts consider it important that students who are on a college track, as well as some in vocational areas, take at least one chemistry course.

Because chemistry is considered a fundamental field and is widely required, a continuing demand exists for men and women qualified to teach it. This means that teaching chemistry is a promising career path for those with the right inclinations.

Chemistry teachers do more than stand at a blackboard lecturing about the periodic table. Here are just some of the responsibilities of teachers and professors:

- Using various teaching methods to instruct students

- Using audiovisual aids to supplement presentations

- Preparing course objectives and outlines

- Demonstrating laboratory experiments

- Supervising students in using laboratory equipment and conducting experiments

- Assigning readings, lab reports, papers, and other student work

- Creating and administering tests

- Evaluating student work and assigning grades

- Advising students

- Participating in committees and professional assignments

- Performing public or community service

- Reviewing potential textbooks and instructional support materials

- Revising and updating curricula

- Participating in professional development functions

- Maintaining course and student records

- Reading and keeping current

For those who teach chemistry at the college or high school level, responsibilities include keeping up with changes in the field, and to a lesser extent keeping current in related fields such as biology and physics. Rapid changes in our understanding of the physical world make it a challenge to keep pace, even with the knowledge and experience of seasoned teachers. But to provide students with a valid educational experience, effective teachers and professors take on this responsibility as a part of their professional commitment.

Obviously, teaching is not for everyone. But are you a good communicator? Do you feel you might have the potential to share your knowledge of chemistry with others in an effective manner? If so, this is a career area worth considering.

Some job titles in this career path follow.

POSSIBLE JOB TITLES

Adjunct (or part-time) faculty member (college)

Assistant professor of chemical engineering (college)

Assistant professor of chemistry (college)

Associate professor of chemistry (college)

Graduate teaching assistant (college)

Instructor of chemistry (college)

Lecturer (college)

Professor of chemistry (college)

Teacher, high school (chemistry)

Teacher, high school (natural sciences)

Teacher, middle school (science)

POSSIBLE EMPLOYERS

Those who want to teach chemistry can take any of several directions. One approach is to become a professor at a four-year college or university. Another path is to teach in a community, junior, or technical college. Still another possibility is to become a teacher at the high school level.

Four-Year Colleges and Universities

For many students who major in chemistry, teaching at the university or four-year college level is a primary goal. Because almost every college and university offers courses in chemistry, a continuing demand exists for faculty with the appropriate training and credentials to teach in this field. While job openings are not always plentiful, the long-term need for qualified chemistry instructors is virtually assured.

After all, more than 2,000 four-year colleges and universities operate in the United States and Canada today. Although not all offer undergraduate majors in chemistry, many do. Some also offer master's or doctoral programs.

Most chemistry faculty at the university level function in two different ways. First, they teach general courses such as General Chemistry or Inorganic Chemistry. This may include teaching students from a wide range of backgrounds who do not intend to major in chemistry (or perhaps any other scientific field). Second, they teach courses designed for students majoring in chemistry or other fields such as biology, physics, and geology.

University faculty also conduct research in a specialized area in which they hold interest. Here are some examples of research-related activities a chemistry professor might undertake in a university setting:

- Developing and implementing research plans

- Writing a grant proposal to the National Science Foundation or other funding agency

- Designing and setting up laboratory experiments

- Replicating research efforts

- Supervising the work of graduate students or other lab personnel

- Documenting research results

- Writing computer programs related to research efforts

- Discussing research problems with colleagues and students

- Reading journals and consulting other sources of research-relayed information

- Communicating with researchers at other institutions via mail, E-mail, telephone, or other means

In the last decade, the college teaching profession has taken a lot of criticism. For example, the concept of tenure, where faculty earn protected job status that may last the rest of their lives, is viewed with resentment by some. Critics outside of higher education contend that professors do not work hard enough and that they enjoy too many privileges compared to other workers in our society.

Actually, this is seldom the case. Teaching at the college level is a demanding profession. Professors must not only give lectures and perform other teaching duties, but they are also expected to conduct research, write articles and books, and perform public service, among other duties. They also advise students, serve on committees, develop and refine courses, and spend a great deal of time simply keeping up in their fields.

While this type of work can be challenging, it is also considered by many as one of the most desirable careers available. Higher-education faculty put in shorter work years than most other workers. They enjoy interesting work environments, and working hours that vary from the 9 to 5 routines of much of the business world. In many ways, teaching chemistry in a university or four-year college can be a great career path.

Two-Year Colleges

While they may not offer chemistry majors, most two-year colleges (known variously as community, junior, and technical colleges) also offer courses in chemistry. Students who plan to transfer to four-year schools can take them as part of their associate degree program. Other students also may take a chemistry course or two as part of their program in nursing or other health-related areas. Chemistry courses may also meet general-studies requirements or be taken as electives. The result is that a demand exists for faculty to teach chemistry courses in two-year colleges around the United States and Canada.

Some community college faculty specialize in chemistry and teach only in that discipline. Occasionally, if they have the necessary credentials, faculty teach a second subject such as mathematics or a second scientific field such as physics or biology. Generally this means having completed sufficient courses at the graduate level in both disciplines to meet accrediting-agency requirements.

To be sure, teaching in two-year colleges is a viable career option for chemistry majors who are willing to earn a master's degree or doctorate.

What is the major difference in community college teaching and other college instruction? Most faculty would cite the course load. Faculty teaching in universities may teach as few as two or three courses per semester. For two-year college faculty, it's more typical to teach five courses per semester.

The difference in course loads means community college faculty spend more time in class than those teaching in universities. They also tend to devote correspondingly more time to grading papers, preparing lectures, and other instructional tasks. Faculty in two-year schools also tend to spend significant amounts of time advising students, serving on college committees, and performing other duties. They do all of this without the help of graduate students or teaching assistants.

All this activity leaves little time for research or publishing. But unlike university faculty, those teaching in two-year colleges are not generally expected to make this a routine part of their jobs. They are viewed as professional teachers rather than researchers, and so are not generally involved in research on any large-scale basis.

Employers of College Teachers: The Numbers

According to the U.S. Department of Education, more than 3,700 colleges and universities operate in the United States today. Thus, even in competitive situations, large numbers of teaching jobs exist.

- ❏ Number of four-year colleges and universities: 2,244

- ❏ Number of two-year institutions: 1,462

OBTAINING COLLEGE TEACHING JOBS

It takes an aggressive approach to obtain a job teaching chemistry, especially at the college level. Although jobs can be found, chances are that for any given opening, a significant number of candidates will apply. This means that to be successful, you must take advantage of the various sources of information about job openings.

Professional Organizations

Chemistry majors and graduates can garner important assistance from professional organizations. Such groups are often a good source of information for locating and pursuing job openings. The networking that takes place through professional organizations can also lead to success in obtaining a job.

Publications

Publications that list job openings in teaching are another source of vital information. It can be well worth your time to look through such publications. Not only do they provide helpful background information, but they can serve as a direct source of information about available jobs.

The Chronicle of Higher Education. Anyone interested in identifying teaching opportunities at the college level should consider consulting *The Chronicle of Higher Education.* This excellent publication includes extensive job listings in every issue. A single issue of the *Chronicle* might include hundreds of job openings in colleges throughout the United States as well as in Canada and other countries, including some in chemistry.

Following are some chemistry teaching positions appearing over a two-week period in the *Chronicle*:

❏ A tenure-track position at a large public university located in the southern United States

❏ A temporary teaching position at a small, church-related college in the Midwest

❏ Two research positions at a major national research laboratory

❏ A full-time teaching position at a West Coast community college

Along with job listings, the *Chronicle* publishes a wide variety of information about higher education, including book reviews, editorials, and in-depth stories about current issues in education, research trends, education financing, professional issues, and other matters. For those who work in higher education or who aspire to employment in academe, it provides fascinating reading and helpful background.

The Chronicle of Higher Education is published on a weekly basis except for the third week in August and the last two weeks of December. It is available in college and university libraries and some public libraries, and through subscription at the following address:

The Chronicle of Higher Education
1255 23rd Street NW
Washington, D.C. 20037

Community College Week. As a publication targeted specifically toward employees at two-year colleges, this publication is helpful in locating job openings in community, junior, and technical colleges. A section of classified ads for positions at various institutions is included. Although job listings are not as extensive as those in *The Chronicle of Higher Education*, they are valuable for those interested in pursuing teaching jobs in two-year colleges. To obtain a copy or subscribe, write to:

Community College Week
10520 Warwick Avenue, Suite B-8
Fairfax, VA 22030-3136

Professional Contacts

Your professors from graduate school, undergraduate professors, and college placement offices can also be helpful in the job search process. Their assistance can be useful in obtaining letters of recommendation, locating part-time or temporary teaching positions, and networking with potential employers.

SALARIES EARNED BY CHEMISTRY PROFESSORS

In 1997–98, college professors earned average salaries as outlined below, according to the American Association of University Professors. For each subsequent year, an increase of 3 to 5 percent would be a reasonable estimate.

	PUBLIC	PRIVATE
Average of all ranks	$53,594	$61,508
Instructor	$32,359	$34,487
Assistant professor	$42,402	$44,946
Associate professor	$51,181	$54,498
Professor	$68,018	$81,752

It is important to keep in mind that faculty salaries vary according to factors such as these:

❑ Faculty rank

❑ Credentials

❑ Longevity

❑ Type/level of institution

❑ Geographical area

Also, private institutions vary in salary structures. The private college figures above are for independent colleges. Church-related colleges and universities tend to have lower salaries than independent schools.

Training and Qualifications

To teach chemistry in college, a bachelor's degree is just the starting point. About the only way a bachelor's grad can teach chemistry is as a teaching assistant while pursuing a graduate degree. For other positions, a master's degree is the minimum requirement. Many positions require a doctorate.

Unlike teaching in high school or middle school, teaching at the college level does not require completion of teacher education courses. Instead, the minimum requirement is a master's degree earned in chemistry, or a master's degree in another field with a significant number of graduate courses in chemistry.

Exact requirements for minimum credentials vary with the type of institution and the demands of agencies that accredit colleges and universities. The Southern Association of Colleges and Schools, for example, requires that all faculty teaching college-level chemistry courses hold, as a minimum, a master's degree with at least eighteen graduate hours in chemistry. Many community college faculty hold teaching positions with this level of preparation, although some also hold doctorates.

In most four-year colleges and universities, it is generally expected that faculty hold a doctoral degree. Even if not an absolute requirement, this becomes a matter of practicality in the job search process (if thirty-five candidates apply for a position and thirty have doctorates, the chance of landing that job with only a master's degree are obviously limited).

If you want to earn a doctorate, you will need dedication and persistence. It takes several years of full-time study beyond the bachelor's degree to earn a doctoral degree (there is no specific time frame; duration varies). Earning a doctorate means more than just taking additional classes of the same type you have completed as an undergraduate. It also means mastering advanced research methodologies and learning to function as an independent researcher.

An excellent brochure is available to guide you on this subject. "Planning for Graduate Work in Chemistry" is free on request from:

American Chemical Society
Committee on Professional Training
1155 16th Street NW
Washington, D.C. 20036

Planning for Graduate School
Anyone thinking about going on to graduate school and studying chemistry should consider the following strategies.

❑ *Earn good grades, especially in chemistry and related courses.* Not surprisingly, good grades are needed if you plan to pursue an academic career. Generally, the higher your grades, the better. What if you're still in school but your grades could be better? Don't panic; it may not be too late. Most graduate schools will look more closely at the last two years of college and at your major area. If you're already out of school, consider taking a few additional chemistry courses and strive for the best possible grades.

❑ *Take the Graduate Record Examination (GRE).* This is a fairly standard requirement for graduate school admission. If you take the exam and your score is not as high as you'd like, consider retaking the exam. In this case, putting in some advance studying or investing in a test-preparation class can be worthwhile. Also, keep in mind that good grades or other factors can sometimes help offset mediocre scores.

❏ *Identify good sources for letters of recommendation.* Professors and research professionals who know your work will usually be glad to write recommendation letters. In requesting such letters, make sure to provide enough lead time to avoid potential problems in meeting deadlines.

In the process, offer to provide background information that will make writing a letter easier. This could include a list of chemistry courses you have taken or the exact dates and names of course taken under the professor from whom a letter is requested.

❏ *Consider several graduate schools.* Instead of setting your sights on just one school, take some time to check out graduate programs offered by several universities. With a broad range of colleges and universities in the United States and Canada, the odds are on your side of finding at least one school that matches your particular interests and abilities.

TEACHING HIGH SCHOOL

Almost every high school offers courses in chemistry. For those willing to obtain the right credentials and who can function effectively in teaching children, this represents an area of real job potential.

To qualify for teaching at the high school level, a chemistry major must be combined with courses designed to prepare students to become certified as teachers. The exact requirements vary in different states and among different colleges and universities. Generally, the process involves completing courses in teacher education, successfully completing a student teaching experience, and passing standardized examinations.

The usual standard for teaching at the high school level is a bachelor's degree plus certification or licensure to teach. To become licensed, you usually must complete a number of education courses and also pass a comprehensive examination required by the state board of education or equivalent body in which you live or plan to teach.

At one time, preparing to teach chemistry or other high school subjects meant majoring in education (sometimes called teacher education) while also taking courses in chemistry or any other subjects you planned to teach.

Today, many colleges and universities follow a different model. Instead of majoring in education, you major in chemistry (or other chosen discipline) and also take a selection of education courses, including student teaching.

As a chemistry major, you can qualify to teach at the high school level by completing all the requirements for a degree in chemistry, plus completing the education courses required by your college and state. Ideally, this is done concurrently with your other studies. But if you're near the end of your bachelor's degree or have already completed it and then decide to pursue a secondary teaching career, you will need to go back and complete these education requirements.

Some colleges offer an alternative approach in which holders of a bachelor's degree complete a special program that brings you in compliance with the necessary requirements. For example, Keene State College in New Hampshire offers a postbaccalaureate teacher certification program. This program allows liberal arts graduates to become certified teachers. Another approach is to earn a master's degree in education, completing teacher certification requirements in the process. Typical course requirements for licensure to teach (varies by institution) include:

Accommodations for Exceptional Learners

Education in the United States

Evaluation of Learning

Introduction to Educational Media

Management of Instruction

The School and the Student

Secondary Curriculum and Instructional Techniques

Student Teaching

CHALLENGES OF HIGH SCHOOL TEACHING

The high school environment is very different from college. Teaching at that level brings its own challenges and responsibilities. Along with time spent on in-class teaching, grading papers, and performing related instructional work, working as a high school chemistry teacher can mean performing tasks such as the following:

- Performing hall or bus duty
- Eating lunch with students and supervising their behavior
- Serving as an advisor to a student club or organization
- Disciplining unruly students
- Driving students to extracurricular activities (such as a science fair)
- Chaperoning at a dance
- Meeting with parents on a routine basis

- Meeting with parents when a student is experiencing or creating special problems

- Serving on an accreditation self-study team

- Serving on a committee to hire a new teacher or administrator

- Ordering textbooks, software, or lab supplies

- Coordinating science fairs

Following is a listing of skills high school teachers need for success (adapted from requirements at Radford University, Radford, Virginia).

- Planning, implementing, and evaluating instruction

- Managing classroom and administrative tasks

- Collecting and interpreting student data

- Promoting students' cognitive, psychomotor, and socioaffective development

- Providing for individual and cultural differences

- Applying knowledge of social forces that affect professional responsibility in a global society

- Working with others in conducting professional tasks and in pursuing professional development

- Applying a breadth and depth of knowledge of the teaching specialty area

TEACHER SALARIES

Teacher salaries can be impressive or disappointing depending on how you look at them. Many teachers complain about unattractive salaries, and they have a point. Compared to earnings of many other professionals, teacher pay is low. For example, an industrial researcher or chemical sales professional may earn substantially more than a high school chemistry teacher.

But at the same time, salaries are not really that bad. In an era when many college graduates find it difficult to find jobs following graduation, a job in teaching offers solid if unspectacular pay as well as good benefits such as health insurance and retirement plans.

In addition, teachers enjoy more time off than most other workers. Most work under nine- or ten-month contracts, providing for significant time off in the summer as well as during holidays. Many teachers use this time to pursue part-time jobs, run their own businesses, or otherwise supplement their income. They may also take advantage of this time to attend graduate school, travel, or pursue other personal interests.

Normally, salary levels for teachers are determined at the local level. Most school districts follow a structured salary schedule based on education and years spent on the job.

Teachers in Virginia, for example, earned the following minimum salaries in 1997–98, with actual salaries varying from one school division to the next and with individual salary increases received in previous years. Other states offer comparable salaries, although actual figures vary.

> Minimum salary, bachelor's degree: $25,272
> Minimum salary, bachelor's plus five years'
>   experience: $27,157
> Minimum salary, master's degree: $27,157

With additional years of experience, salaries move up into the 30s and 40s, and some senior teachers earn more than $50,000 annually.

Comparable salaries are earned by teachers in other states, with higher salaries the norm in major cities and areas where living costs are higher.

On average, teachers in private high schools tend to earn salaries that are somewhat lower than those paid public school teachers. Actual salaries vary from one school to the next.

OBTAINING HIGH SCHOOL AND MIDDLE SCHOOL TEACHING JOBS

The process of obtaining a teaching position in a middle school or high school usually involves more of a local emphasis than does the college hiring process. While most colleges advertise regionally or nationally for full-time vacancies, the typical school district relies more on local or statewide advertising. Thus, a good way to learn about openings is to consult the classified sections of newspapers.

An increasingly productive way to seek out teaching jobs is to use the Internet. Many school districts now post information about their schools, and sometimes about job openings, on the Internet.

An outstanding example is EDNET, a free online service that lists teaching openings. From its base in Woodland Hills, California, this service posts the following:

❑ Job openings in Southern California schools

❑ Selected openings in other parts of California, and in other states

❑ A list of California's school districts

Other similar services may be available for your area or for states or regions in which you're interested. To locate them, just use any Internet search engine and seek out "teaching jobs" or similar identifiers.

Another strategy is to contact school districts directly. Ask for a list of any anticipated job openings, and submit a resume or application.

Some prospective teachers use substitute teaching as a way to get started. Often, those who have served as substitutes become a "known quantity" and may gain an edge when full-time positions become available.

EDUCATIONAL ADMINISTRATION

Teaching is not the only professional option once you start an educational career. A closely related area is educational administration. Every school and college has administrators who manage its academic affairs as well as other areas ranging from executive management to administrative support.

Most typically, administrators in the educational setting start out as teachers. They then progress to administrative roles. In the middle school or high school setting, a teacher interested in administrative work might take on such a role as assistant principal. This usually requires completion of additional classes or a degree in educational administration, coupled with sufficient teaching experience. After spending some time as an assistant principal, an administrator might move on to a principal's position, and from there to a central office position such as curriculum coordinator, director of pupil services, or assistant superintendent of schools. A relatively few administrators might eventually assume top-level roles such as superintendent of schools or state-level positions such as state superintendent of schools.

Administrators also hold a large number of jobs at the college level. In higher education, no specific training in administration is necessarily required. Faculty tend to learn on the job once they are appointed to administrative positions, such as the role of department chairperson. In some cases, faculty who aspire to administrative jobs complete master's or doctoral degrees in administrative or management fields.

It is not uncommon for faculty to accept administrative roles temporarily and then return to teaching. In other cases, those who start out as faculty members become career administrators. They may go on to hold positions such as dean, vice president, or college president.

Following are some typical job titles for educational administrators.

JOB TITLES IN EDUCATIONAL ADMINISTRATION

Public School Administrative Positions

Assistant principal	Director of instruction
Assistant superintendent of schools	Director of transportation
Associate superintendent of schools	Principal
Director of curriculum	Superintendent of schools
Director of finance and administration	

College and University Administrative Positions

Assistant to the president	Director of planning
Associate vice president	Division chairperson
Dean, College of Arts and Sciences	President
Dean of instruction	Provost
Dean of student services	Registrar
Department chairperson	Vice president for academic affairs
Director of enrollment management	Vice president for administration
Director of institutional advancement	Vice president for advancement
Director of institutional research	

RELATED CAREERS

In addition to educational administration, a chemistry major can also lead to other career paths related to teaching. The skills used in the classroom are not unlike those used in a number of other occupations. Consider the following job titles as a beginning list. Then investigate these and other positions that draw on the skill base you have developed.

Corporate trainer

Educational consultant

Researcher

Sales representative, educational
publishing company

Textbook editor

Textbook writer

Tutor

Web page developer

PROFESSIONAL ASSOCIATIONS FOR CHEMISTRY TEACHERS, PROFESSORS, AND RELATED PROFESSIONALS

American Chemical Society
1155 16th Street NW
Washington, D.C. 20036
Members/Purpose: Serves more than 150,000 members, including teachers and professors of chemistry.
Journals/Publications: *Journal of the American Chemical Society*; *Chemical and Engineering News*; *ChemTech*; many other publications.
Training: Provides courses, seminars, and workshops.
Job Listings: Offers career guidance counseling.

American Association for the Advancement of Science
1200 New York Avenue NW
Washington, D.C. 20005
Members/Purpose: Serves more than 140,000 working scientists, college and university faculty, K–12 teachers, students, and others.
Journal/Publication: *Science.*
Training: Meetings and other conferences.
Job Listings: Holds an annual career fair helping match job candidates and employers.

American Association of University Professors
1012 14th Street NW, Suite 500
Washington, D.C. 20005
Members/Purpose: Serves college and university faculty.
Journal/Publications: *Academe*; also publishes annual faculty salary report.
Training: Meetings and other conferences.

National Association of Professional Educators
412 1st Street NE
Washington, D.C. 20000

Members/Purpose: Serves as an alternative to teacher unions. Membership includes 75,000 professional educators.
Journal/Publication: *Professional Education Newsletter.*
Training: Annual meeting.

National Education Association
1201 16th Street NW
Washington, D.C. 20036
Members/Purpose: Professional organization advancing the cause of public education. More than 2.2 million members represent all areas of education, from preschool to graduate programs.
Journals/Publications: *NEA Today*; *NEA Focus.*
Training: Meetings and conferences.

CHAPTER 12

PATH 3: CHEMICAL ENGINEERING

S ome students who start out majoring in engineering are also interested in chemistry, and decide to specialize in chemical engineering. Some who begin as potential chemistry majors decide to major in chemical engineering instead. It is also possible for a chemistry major to complete studies in that field, and then pursue an additional degree in chemical engineering. However it is approached, chemical engineering represents a viable career path for those interested in the principles and applications of chemistry.

DEFINITION OF THE CAREER PATH

Chemical engineering is a very broad-based discipline. It includes knowledge from several fields, including physics, biology, and mathematics, as well as chemistry. The work of chemical engineers has applications in diverse areas, ranging from the development of new medicines to ways to produce energy.

While the typical chemical engineering graduate goes on to work in the field or to undertake related graduate study, other options are also possible. For example, a chemical engineering degree can prepare students for attending medical school, working in business management, or earning a master's degree in business administration.

Chemical engineering has existed as a distinct field for only a little over a century. According to the department of chemical engineering at the

Massachusetts Institute of Technology (MIT), the field has is origins at that school. In 1888, MIT, under the leadership of professor Lewis Norton, was the first to offer an integrated curriculum that combined elements of chemistry, mechanical engineering, and related knowledge. Since that time, it has grown into a diverse and widely utilized field. Much of the modern growth of the petroleum and chemical industries has been a direct result of the development of the field of chemical engineering.

Chemical engineers work for a wide variety of industries and other employers. These include several major areas identified by the American Institute of Chemical Engineers as outlined below.

Chemical Process Industry

A major area of employment for chemical engineers is the chemical process industry. In this work, they design and operate processes and systems for handling, transporting, combining, separating, and storing chemical products. This ranges from agricultural chemicals and paper products to paints, soaps, detergents, and specialty chemicals.

Biotechnology Industry

Unlike most other areas employing chemical engineers, this industry is based on biological research and techniques. Chemical engineers who work in biotechnology design processes for conducting research. They also develop products derived from living organisms.

Electronics Industry

Chemical engineers provide important support to the electronics industry. They design process control equipment and develop materials used in production of electronic components. Engineers also plan and support the manufacturing of microchips and electronic circuits.

Food and Beverages Industry

Manufacturing and processing food on a large scale requires efficient processes. Chemical engineers help design such processes. This includes ensuring safe handling and preparation of food, developing new products, and designing new types of packaging and storage.

Advanced Materials Industries

Chemical engineers help develop new materials that can be used in the aerospace, automotive, and metallurgical industries, among others. For example, they might develop improved ceramics to take the place of metal used in airplanes or space vehicles.

Design and Construction Industry

Chemical engineers play a key role in the design and construction industry. They design and build facilities, equipment, and processes. Their efforts support manufacturing, production, and other functions. Much of their work emphasizes safe operations as well as efficient practices.

Fuel Industries

Many chemical engineers work in fuel-related industries, including natural gas production, petroleum production and refining, and development of synthetic fuels. Some also work with nuclear energy and alternative energy sources such as biomass and solar energy.

Environmental Safety and Health

An important area of chemical engineering is that of safety, health, and environmental protection. Since the production of chemicals can generate harmful byproducts, it is important to see that they do not damage people or the environment. Chemical engineers develop and improve processes for enhancing safety in the chemical industry, both for employees and the public at large. They also deal with wastewater management and other types of waste management, as well as finding practical use for wastes or chemical byproducts.

Thus one chemical engineer might work to improve food processing techniques and methods of producing fertilizers, while another might develop more efficient methods of refining petroleum products. Others might help develop synthetic fibers for use in making clothing, assist in processing industrial chemicals, develop ways to mass-produce prescription drugs, or formulate solutions to environmental problems.

JOB TITLES FOR CHEMICAL ENGINEERS

Along with the general title of "chemical engineer," workers in this field have job titles such as the following:

Biomedical specialist	Consultant
Compliance officer	Environmental engineer
Computer allocations engineer	Environmental specialist

Manufacturing production engineer

Plant manager

Plant process engineer

Process design engineer

Process safety engineer

Product engineer

Project engineer

Project manager

Quality control engineer

Regulatory affairs engineer

Research and development engineer

Technical manager

Technical services engineer

Specialty Areas

Chemical engineering majors may choose from a variety of special areas not just during their studies, but in the employment arena. For example, students at the Massachusetts Institute of Technology (MIT) study specialty areas such as the following:

Biochemical engineering

Biomedical engineering

Catalysis and chemical kinetics

Colloid science and separations

Energy engineering

Environmental engineering

Materials

Polymers

Process systems engineering

Thermodynamics, statistical mechanics, and molecular simulation

Transport processes

Other universities offer similar specialties, and working engineers often specialize in areas such as these.

The trend toward interdisciplinary work bodes well for those interested in exciting fields such as biotechnology. Chemical engineers of the future won't be restricted to working in chemical or petroleum manufacturing. They may also work in areas such as biotechnology. For example, MIT offers a program in metabolic engineering. This combines offerings of the departments of chemical engineering and biology, focusing on the improvement of cellular properties and function through advanced biochemical reactions.

Most chemical engineers work in one of these fields of specialization identified by the American Institute of Chemical Engineers:

Biotechnology

Ceramics

Electronic components and chemicals

Environmental control and clean-up   Pulp and paper

Food   Safety engineering

Petrochemicals   Textiles

Pharmaceuticals

Research Areas

Even though chemical engineering may be seen as a more "practical" field than chemistry, some jobs involve specializing in research. Research specialists work in universities, commercial laboratories, government agencies, and elsewhere. Examples of research areas include:

Biocatalysis and bioreactors   Genetic and metabolic engineering

Chemical process control   Heat transfer

Fluid particles and fluid particle   Intracellular and extracellular
  systems   monitoring methods

Forest products industries   Transport properties

POSSIBLE EMPLOYERS

Some chemical engineers are self-employed, working as consultants or other specialists. But the great majority are employed by corporations, government agencies, educational institutions, or other organizations. Employers of chemical engineers include:

Aerospace firms   Environmental engineering firms

Agricultural chemical companies   Food manufacturers and processors

Atomic Energy Commission   Glass manufacturers

Beverage manufacturers   Hazardous waste removal companies

Biotechnology firms   Metallurgical companies

Ceramics manufacturers   National Aeronautics and Space
                                           Administration
Chemical equipment manufacturers
                                         Nuclear fuel producers
Construction companies
                                         Nuclear Regulatory Commission
Electronics companies
                                         Oil and gas companies

Paint manufacturers	Textile manufacturers
Petroleum refineries	U.S. Army
Photographic products	U.S. Department of Agriculture
Professional associations	U.S. Department of Commerce
Pulp and paper manufacturers	U.S. Department of Energy
Rubber processing firms	U.S. Environmental Protection Agency
Soap and detergent manufacturers	
Specialty chemical firms	U.S. Navy
State environmental management agencies	Waste treatment facilities

TRAINING AND QUALIFICATIONS

Chemistry majors who are interested in the engineering side of things may take engineering courses while still undergraduates. Or they can go on to study chemical engineering at the graduate level after having completed a bachelor's degree with a major in chemistry.

For example, students with backgrounds in chemistry or other science disciplines may be admitted to the master's degree program in chemical engineering offered by Montana State University. The MSU Department of Chemical Engineering offers graduate programs with concentrations in several areas. This includes a traditional chemical engineering program (with or without a thesis), a program for nonchemical engineering undergraduates that includes a limited remedial component, a materials research program, and an environmental engineering program. The department also offers doctoral programs with emphases in traditional chemical engineering, biofilms and biotechnology, materials and the applied mechanics of materials, and environmental engineering.

The master's programs require twenty-two semester course credits plus at least ten thesis credits, or thirty-two course credits for non-thesis plans, plus an overall examination. In addition, the traditional chemical engineering program for students from other disciplines requires some background remedial coursework.

For a doctorate in chemical engineering, students earn about twenty course credits beyond the master's level, plus a minimum of eighteen thesis credits in addition to a qualifying examination, oral comprehensive examinations, and a final examination and thesis defense.

Typical Engineering Courses

The chemical engineering courses available at Montana State are typical of college programs in this field. They include the following, ranging from freshman-level to doctoral courses:

Advanced Composite Materials

Advanced Engineering Analysis I

Advanced Engineeering Materials

Advanced Fluid Mechanics I

Bioprocess Engineering

Catalysis and Applied Surface Chemistry

Chemical Engineering Laboratory

Chemical Engineering Seminar

Chemical Equilibrium

Chemical Reaction Engineering

Composite Materials

Computations in Chemical Engineering

Cooperative Internship

Design Case Studies

Design of Chemical and Petroleum Processes I

Design of Chemical and Petroleum Processes II

Doctoral Thesis

Elementary Principles I

Elementary Principles II

Failure of Materials

Fluid Mechanics and Heat Transfer

Freshman Seminar

Graduate Consultation

Hazardous Waste Management

Individual Problems

Internship

Introduction to Polymer Engineering

Mass Transfer

Mass Transfer Operations

Master's Thesis

Materials Science

Numerical Solutions to Engineering Problems

Process Control

Process Dynamics and Control

Reaction Engineering and Reaction Modeling

Separations

Societal Impacts of Chemical Engineering

Special Topics

Surface Engineering

Thermodynamics

Transport Analysis

Undergraduate Research/Creative Activity Instruction

Undergraduate Thesis

Viscous Fluid Dynamics

Other colleges and universities offer similar programs. Larger institutions tend to have more specialty areas from which to choose; check with any school in which you're interested to find out what is available.

Applying to Graduate School

If you're a chemistry major or recent graduate and decide to shoot for a master's or higher degree in chemical engineering, chemistry, or another field, the first step is applying for admission to graduate school. Most graduate schools require the following from applicants:

1. A completed application for graduate admission. This is available on request from any university.

2. An application fee. The amount varies, but $25 to $50 is typical. Some schools do not require an application fee.

3. Letters of recommendation. Usually, these are from professors who know your work.

4. Transcripts of your college credits and grades.

5. Test scores. Your scores from the Graduate Record Examination (GRE) will be a necessary part of the application package.

For more information about planning for graduate school, see the booklet "Planning for Graduate Work in Chemistry," published by the American Chemical Society's committee on professional training. For a copy, write to:

American Chemical Society
1155 16th Street NW
Washington, D.C. 20026

EARNINGS

Chemical engineers earn good pay. According to the American Institute of Chemical Engineers, the median entry-level salary for a bachelor's degree is $43,000. This is a beginning salary, so you can see that chemical engineering is a well-paying field. It ranks far ahead of the great majority of career fields outside of engineering or the professions. Engineers with master's degrees and those with more experience tend to earn even higher salaries.

In government jobs (see chart in Chapter 10, page 125), salary ranges follow strict guidelines established by the government. In the private sector, salaries have more room for difference. In either setting, salaries are excellent.

WORKING CONDITIONS

Working conditions for chemical engineers are similar to those of chemists, but with less emphasis on the laboratory and more on field operations. Their work may take place in offices, in the production areas of chemical plants, in laboratories, or in classrooms.

At one point, an engineer's work might consist of sitting in front of a desktop computer, working in a comfortable, well-maintained office. Another time, it might mean climbing a three-story distillation tower to get a firsthand look at a production problem.

In fact, work settings for chemical engineers vary a great deal. Engineers work in their own offices and those of colleagues, in conference rooms, in law libraries, and other locations. Generally, such locations are quite comfortable, with all the trappings one would expect of modern offices. For those who are just getting started or who work for government or "no frills," though, office settings may be quite modest. They may be small, cramped, and simply appointed. At the other extreme, some chemical engineers may enjoy large, attractive offices.

Outside of offices and lab facilities, chemical engineers may perform a variety of field work, depending on job assignments and the nature of work in which they specialize. For example, an engineer employed in the petroleum industry may spend significant time working in refineries. Another who works in environmental management might put in time at a wastewater treatment plant or a site where hazardous waste is being removed. Working conditions in other specialty areas may vary similarly.

FINDING JOBS

How do you find a job in chemical engineering? A great starting point is to use the processes established by universities to help their graduates find jobs. These processes vary from one school to another, but virtually all colleges and universities view helping graduates find jobs as one of their responsibilities, and provide services accordingly.

Typically, assistance in helping students includes services such as the following:

- ❏ Job fairs and employer visits where prospective employers come to the campus and interview students who will be graduating during that academic year

- ❏ Help in scheduling on-campus interviews on an individualized basis

❑ Assistance in scheduling off-campus interviews

❑ Correspondence with prospective employers and posting of job openings on bulletin boards, Web pages, and other sites

❑ Publication of lists of job openings

❑ Individualized counseling and advisement regarding the career search process

Some private companies provide information about job openings. In many cases, there is no fee to the job applicant; instead, employers pay these companies to find employees for them. You can locate such firms on the Internet or in your phone book's yellow pages.

For example, North Technical Search of Sussex, Wisconsin specializes in engineering, management, and skilled technical positions in the automotive, metal casting, foundry, and manufacturing industries. The company is also a member of several job recruiting networks and can offer job possibilities in other countries as well as the United States.

At any one time, it is not unusual to have thirty or more positions in chemistry or chemical engineering listed by this firm. For more information, contact:

North Technical Search
N90 W25279 Tomahawk Drive
Sussex, WI 53089

The company also operates a Web site and can be contacted online. Other companies in other locations offer similar services.

RELATED OCCUPATIONS

Occupations related to chemical engineering include the following:

Biomedical engineer	Engineering technician
Chemical engineering professor	Environmental chemist
Chemist	Environmental engineer
Consultant	Quality control chemist
Engineering school dean	Technical writer

PROFESSIONAL ASSOCIATIONS FOR CHEMICAL ENGINEERS

American Chemical Society
1155 16th Street NW
Washington, D.C. 20036
Members/Purpose: Serves more than 150,000 members as a broad-based society for chemists and chemical engineers.
Journals/Publications: *Journal of the American Chemical Society; Chemical and Engineering News; ChemTech;* many other publications.
Training: Provides courses, seminars, and workshops.
Job Listings: Offers career guidance counseling.

American Institute of Chemical Engineers
United Engineering Center
345 East 47th Street
New York, NY 10017
Members/Purpose: Fifty-eight thousand chemical engineers in industry, academia, and government. Members include engineers and supporters of engineering at all levels including students, practicing engineers, and managers.
Journals/Publications: *Chemical Engineering Progress,* a monthly magazine for CPI professionals; *AIChE Journal,* a peer-reviewed monthly journal; *Environmental Progress; Process Safety Progress.*
Training: Holds two major conferences each year, including the annual meeting; sponsors specialized topical conferences, meetings, and expositions. Also offers a modular instruction series for self-study.

Canadian Society for Chemical Engineering
130 Slater Street
Ottawa, Ontario
Canada K1P 6E2
Members/Purpose: Serves chemical engineers in Canada.
Journals/Publications: *Canadian Journal of Chemical Engineering; Directory of Chemical Engineering Research in Canada.*
Training: Holds two conferences and workshops; holds biennial student conference; sponsors student chapters.

Society of Plastics Engineers
P.O. Box 403
Brookfield, CT 06804
Members/Purpose: Promotes knowledge and education related to plastics and polymers. Has twenty technical divisions and ninety-eight local sections.

Journals/Publications: *Plastics Engineering*; other technical publications.
Training: Provides technical conferences, seminars, and workshops, and a
certification program.
Job Listings: Offers online employment network.

The American Nuclear Society
555 North Kensington Avenue
LaGrange Park, IL 60526
Members/Purpose: Approximately 13,000 engineers, scientists, educators,
and administrators.
Journals/Publications: *Nuclear Science and Engineering, Nuclear
Technology*, and *Fusion Technology*; other publications.

American Petroleum Institute
1220 L Street NW
Washington, D.C. 20005
Members/Purpose: Serves as a forum for all parts of the oil and natural
gas industry; pursues public policy objectives; advances interests of the
industry.
Journals/Publications: Various booklets and technical publications;
newsletter, *API Reports*.
Training: Offers seminars, workshops, and symposia; provides training
materials.

Materials Research Society
506 Keystone Drive
Warrendale, PA 15086
Members/Purpose: Promotes basic and applied research on materials of
technological importance. Members include scientists and engineers from
industry, education, and government.
Journals/Publications: *Journal of Materials Research*; newsletter.
Training: Holds conferences.

CHAPTER 13

PATH 4: SCIENCE MANAGEMENT AND SUPPORT

W hile the typical chemistry major might envision a future career in teaching or research, another area of potential employment is often overlooked: working as a manager or sales professional, or in another support capacity. Given the extensive nature of the chemical industry and the research enterprise in the United States and Canada, the need for personnel to manage and support various functions is extensive.

DEFINITION OF THE CAREER PATH

In any organization employing more than just a few people, the need for managers arises. This is as true in a research organization as it is in an industrial concern. Someone needs to supervise workers, set goals, manage budgets, and take care of numerous other details inherent in operating any organization. Such roles include positions such as laboratory supervisors, research directors, plant managers, and other management roles.

In business and industry, where the ultimate goal is to make a profit, sales staff are also needed to market the company's products. Chemical sales professionals fill this role.

Chemical technicians and workers filling other support roles also perform tasks necessary to successful research, development, or production.

Science and Industrial Managers

Managers in scientific and technical organizations plan, coordinate, and direct the activities of their organizations. These activities might consist of research, development, design, or production. Managers supervise chemists, chemical engineers, technicians, and a variety of support personnel.

A major task for managers is to determine scientific and technical goals and to work with staff in carrying them out. They also manage the day-to-day operations of laboratories, production units, or other facilities.

Science managers oversee activities such as experimentation, testing, quality control, and production. They may be involved in their own research in addition to managing the work of others. Other typical tasks include the following:

- Hiring new staff

- Evaluating existing staff

- Making job assignments

- Developing concepts for new projects and identifying ways to address problems encountered during project completion

- Developing and managing budgets

- Supervising the purchase of equipment, materials, and supplies

- Evaluating the progress of work undertaken and providing leadership for continuous improvement

- Coordinating work with other units performing related activities

- Keeping senior managers informed through written and oral reports

In the industrial or research setting, managers often draw on their own scientific knowledge and experience in completing their duties. Many managers were initially trained as chemists or engineers and then moved into management positions at some later point in their careers. Such positions also represent a viable career goal for chemistry majors or recent graduates as they look ahead.

Serving in scientific management or support can take on a variety of forms. Some jobs consist of providing overall administrative duties for a lab or other facility. Others include both mid-level positions and top-level executive management positions such as a president or vice president of a company or one of its divisions. A common job title in this area is director of research. Other titles are shown below.

POSSIBLE JOB TITLES

Assistant plant manager

Associate research director

Coordinator of research

Director of research and
    development

Laboratory coordinator

Laboratory supervisor

Operations manager

Plant manager

President

Quality control manager

Research director

Vice president

Chemical Sales

If you understand chemistry but don't want to work in research or production, an entirely different option is to consider a sales career. The area of chemical sales covers a number of job possibilities. Sales professionals are a key component of the chemical business and related industries.

Chemical sales may involve the sale of raw materials or of finished products. Here are just some of the materials you might find yourself marketing as a chemical sales professional:

Air fresheners

Bonding agents for plaster and
    concrete

Curing agents

Defoamers

Detergents

Disinfectants and sanitizers

Insecticides

Metal oxides

Polishes, waxes, and strippers

Pulp and paper products

Solvent-based resins

Specialty polymers

Thickeners

Water treatment chemicals

Sales Areas

The Chemical Marketing and Research Association has identified the following general job areas within the chemical industry and related industries:

Acquisitions and mergers

Commercial development

Consulting

Investment/financial analysis

Licensing	Planning
Marketing	Product management
Marketing research	Purchasing
New ventures	Sales

For some of the jobs in these areas, an academic background in chemistry is ideal. For others, a business background is needed. In many cases, a combination of chemistry and business (for example, a bachelor's degree in chemistry and a master's in business administration) is best.

Sales and management positions can also be found in a variety of specialized companies related to the chemical industry. For example, the Canadian Manufacturers of Chemical Specialties Association has identified the following specialties for companies that make up its membership:

Aerosols	Flame retarding chemicals
Antimicrobial chemicals	Pest control products
Antiseptics	Sanitizers
Automotive chemicals	Soaps and detergents
Deodorizers	Water treatment chemicals
Disinfectants	Waxes and polishes

Sales jobs can be multifaceted. At Dow, for example, sales representatives function as technical and financial consultants with customers. Part of their job is to understand the business goals and technical needs of customers. Sales staff attempt to match customer needs with the company's product offerings, in the process demonstrating ways customers can meet their business goals by working with Dow. This work includes maintaining a knowledgeable perspective on market trends and future customer needs.

Chemical Equipment Sales

Another potential career area is that of a sales professional specializing in industrial or laboratory equipment. Chemical companies, research labs, schools, colleges, and other organizations need various types of equipment to conduct their operations. Sales professionals represent the manufacturers of such equipment in selling it on a wholesale or retail basis. Just a small sample of industrial equipment is as follows:

- Heat exchangers
- Water purification equipment

- Distillation equipment
- Coating drums
- Vacuum pumps
- Glass-lined reactors
- Blending mixers
- O-rings
- Bag-filling machines

Examples of laboratory equipment might include:

- Spectrometers
- Chromatographs
- Fume hoods
- Fat and protein analyzers
- Laboratory glassware
- Calorimeters
- Particle size analyzers

Working as a sales professional offers a number of attractive features. Among them are:

- Functioning in a business-to-business sales environment
- Using "people skills" in working with a large number of technical and business contacts, both within one's own companies and with other organizations
- The flexibility to manage one's own time and work without close supervision
- The challenge of holding front-line responsibility for customer satisfaction
- Enjoying the chance to apply hands-on technical knowledge to business and sales needs
- Serving as a part of a sales and/or management team
- Using problem-solving skills
- Seeing new places (in jobs where overnight travel is required)

Chemistry Technicians

Another avenue for chemistry majors is to work as a technician. Many of these jobs do not require completion of a bachelor's degree, but that does not rule them out for students in four-year colleges. In fact, some employers prefer to hire bachelor's degree graduates in technician positions. Also, chemistry majors who have not yet completed a degree may follow this occupational path in part-time or summer employment, or in situations where they decide to take a break from their college studies.

According to the U.S. Department of Labor, job opportunities are expected to be very good in the near future for various types of science technicians, including chemistry technicians.

Technicians work in support of chemists and other scientists. Their work is similar to that of scientists, but tends to be more practical in nature. Chemistry technicians set up laboratory equipment, monitor experiments, maintain equipment, and document results of experiments. Some work in production rather than research. Here, they may assist in quality control, product testing, and working with specialized laboratory and production instrumentation.

POSSIBLE EMPLOYERS

Almost all of the prospective employers of chemists or chemical engineers also represent potential employers for those wishing to work in management, sales, or support. Some of these employers are listed below.

Agricultural products companies

Biotechnology firms

Centers for Disease Control and Prevention

Chemical production plants

Chemical research and development firms

Drug manufacturers

Electronic equipment manufacturers

Environmental management companies

Food and beverage manufacturers

Food and Drug Administration

National Institutes of Health

Paint manufacturers

Paper and pulp manufacturers

Petroleum companies

Plastics manufacturers

Professional organizations

Research laboratories

Rubber processing firms

Soap and detergent manufacturers

Specialty chemical firms

State environmental management
agencies

Textile companies

Universities and colleges

U.S. Department of Agriculture

U.S. Department of Defense

U.S. Department of Health and
Human Services

U.S. Environmental Protection
Agency

Waste treatment facilities

EARNINGS

Salaries earned by managers, sales professionals, and other support personnel vary widely. For a small, newly established business, salaries may lag well behind those more well established. For a large national or multinational corporation, salaries may be quite good, especially for upper-level managers. In addition, fringe benefits can be attractive, and innovative features such as deferred compensation are becoming more common.

According to the U.S. Department of Labor, scientific managers earn average salaries ranging from $45,000 to more than $100,000 annually. Salaries for those in the chemical field vary significantly depending on the type of employer, geographical location, and experience and credentials of the individual. But since many of the positions supervised by managers (such as chemists and chemical engineers) themselves earn excellent salaries, those of managers can be well above the average for all technical and scientific personnel. Those who hold high-level positions may also enjoy expense accounts, stock option plans, bonuses, and other benefits.

For sales personnel, no single average figure is meaningful. Since many sales jobs involve payment of commissions based on sales volume, salaries are often determined by individual initiative and marketing conditions at the time. But in general, sales salaries compare favorably with those earned by lower- and mid-level managers.

The salaries earned by chemical technicians and other support personnel also vary depending on credentials, job duties, and other factors. Most technicians earn between $20,000 and $40,000 per year, according to the U.S. Department of Labor.

TRAINING AND QUALIFICATIONS

In some cases, college-level preparation in business, management, or marketing provides the necessary background for entry-level jobs in science management, sales, or support. Many of the more technical jobs, however, require training in chemistry or chemical engineering. For example, a manager in a research setting would normally have a chemistry degree, perhaps at the master's or doctoral level.

A graduate of a bachelor's degree chemistry program might qualify for entry-level jobs in sales or management. If credentials are also added in a business field, that might strengthen job prospects.

One avenue is to earn a bachelor's degree with a major in chemistry and also complete a second major, or a minor, in business management in a related field. Another is to complete a master's of business administration (M.B.A.) degree. This can open doors in business, industry, and other potential employers.

Some M.B.A. programs are designed specifically for those with scientific or technical backgrounds. For example, Cornell University in Ithaca, New York offers an M.B.A. program for scientists, engineers, and others with scientific or technical credentials. This special twelve-month M.B.A. option offers a selective course of study for people with advanced scientific or technical degrees. The program draws on students' prior analytical training and experience, allowing them to move at an accelerated pace through the quantitative core curriculum and focus on business applications of those skills.

Participants in this innovative program receive fifteen credits of advanced standing for prior graduate work. They complete most of the required course work during an intensive ten-week summer term. They then join the second-year class in the fall and participate in the regular academic-year program. Successful students receive their M.B.A. degree in the spring and can re-enter the workforce after only a one-year break in their career.

The summer term course in this program replaces six separate first-year courses: Financial Accounting, Marketing Management, Microeconomics for Management, Quantitative Methods for Management, Managerial Finance, and Production and Operations Management. Once this intensive course is completed, students select from nearly eighty electives offered by Cornell.

Other M.B.A. programs may not be designed just for science graduates, but can easily be combined with an undergraduate degree in almost any field to add business and management competencies.

Some institutions offer a basic M.B.A. program with little variety. Others offer an assortment of options. The University of Florida, for instance, gives M.B.A. students an abundance of choices. They can choose from six degree options, fourteen concentrations, six joint degree programs, two dual degree programs, and eleven international exchange opportunities. Of special note is the Flexible M.B.A. Program, which combines interactive technology, a weeklong international trip, and eight campus visits over twenty months to provide an M.B.A. degree via the Internet.

Other M.B.A. options available at the University of Florida include:

Accelerated M.B.A. Program

Corporate M.B.A. Program

Executive M.B.A. Programs

Flexible M.B.A. Program

Joint programs with pharmacy, biotechnology, law, and other disciplines

Managers M.B.A. Programs

Traditional M.B.A. Program

STRATEGIES FOR FINDING JOBS

There is no single method for finding jobs in management, sales, or support in the chemistry field. One place to start is your college's career placement office. Be alert for campus visits by representatives of chemical companies and other employers, as well as for postings of job openings with such groups. Then apply for any that interest you.

The classified sections of major newspapers also include ads for jobs with chemical manufacturers, research facilities, and other employers. Newspapers published in smaller cities will include ads for local job openings, but you'll need to consult major papers such as *The New York Times* and *The Washington Post* for regional or national openings.

You can also contact organizations directly and request information on job openings and how you might apply. Some employers now include such information online; you need only check out their site on the World Wide Web.

Other sources of job information include publications targeted specifically toward those who are already employed in the field, professional organizations, and friends or colleagues who are already employed.

Private job search services also provide a good source of employment information. You can locate them online or through the yellow pages or classified ads.

WORKING CONDITIONS

Working conditions in management, sales, and support positions vary widely. For managers and sales personnel, standard office settings can be expected. Surroundings might range from a cubicle with a desk and phone to a large, attractive office. The smaller the organization or the less experienced the worker, the more likely that work settings will be simple.

Sales staff may also be expected to travel frequently. This means a great deal of time might be spent in the offices of customers, as well as in hotel rooms, airplanes, or cars.

Some managers and virtually all technicians also spend time working in laboratories or industrial plants, where they experience the same kinds of conditions as research chemists or production workers.

Many managers work more than forty hours a week. This varies by situation, but can include evening and weekend work when required by the employer or if special projects must be completed.

RELATED OCCUPATIONS

Many of the skills involved in management and sales can be applied in other career areas. Skills such as planning, organizing, communicating, and supervising others can be applied in businesses, industries, large corporations, and other settings. Following are some representative job titles for related career areas.

Account executive	Management consultant
Chemical production worker	Marketing director
Chemist	Office manager
Engineer	Sales manager
Human resources manager	Technical editor

PROFESSIONAL ASSOCIATIONS FOR MANAGERS, SALES PROFESSIONALS, AND RELATED PERSONNEL

American Marketing Association
250 South Wacker Drive, Suite 200
Chicago, IL 60606
Members/Purpose: Forty-five thousand members from more than ninety countries involved in marketing (including sales professionals, managers, and others).
Journals/Publications: *Marketing News* (biweekly magazine); *Journal of Marketing*; *Journal of International Marketing*; *Journal of Public Policy and Marketing*; other publications.

Training: Twenty-five national conferences annually; meetings, seminars, and workshops.

Canadian Chemical Producers Association

350 Sparks Street, Suite 805
Ottawa, Ontario
Canada K1R 7S8
Members/Purpose: Members include more than seventy companies (employing more than 24,000 people) producing inorganic chemicals, petrochemicals, organic and specialty chemicals, and related products. Represents and promotes Canada's chemical industry.
Journals/Publications: Publishes a variety of reports.
Training: Holds conferences.

Canadian Manufacturers of Chemical Specialties Association

56 Sparks Street, Suite 500
Ottawa, Ontario
Canada K1P 5A9
Members/Purpose: Members include companies producing a wide variety of chemical specialty products.
Journals/Publications: *Microgram* (quarterly newsletter); *Formulator* (annual magazine).
Training: Annual conference; training seminars.

Chemical Management & Resources Association

1255 23rd Street NW
Washington, D.C. 20037
Members/Purpose: About 1,000 professionals in the chemical and allied industries; promotes growth and development of chemical and allied process industries.
Journals/Publications: Newsletter; directory; meeting papers.
Training: National technical meetings; special courses and programs; annual business school; annual basic short courses.

Chemical Specialties Manufacturers Association

1913 Eye Street NW
Washington, D.C. 20006
Members/Purpose: Serves more than 400 companies engaged in manufacturing, formulating, distributing, or selling chemical safety products.
Journal/Publication: Quarterly journal, *Chemical Times & Trends*.
Training: Annual conventions; seminars.

National Association of Chemical Distributors
1525 Wilson Boulevard, Suite 750
Arlington, VA 22209
Members/Purpose: More than 330 chemical distributors. Also operates
the Chemical Educational Foundation, which promotes chemical safety,
health, and environmental protection.
Journal/Publication: *Chemical Distributor.*
Training: Annual operations seminar and trade show.

National Association of Sales Professionals
8300 North Hayden Road, Suite 207
Scottsdale, AZ 85258
Members/Purpose: Supports training, education, and developmental needs
of men and women employed full-time in sales.
Journal/Publication: *Nova,* the National Association of Sales Professional's
official newsletter.
Training: Offers NASP Education Institute; sponsors a professional
certification program.

National Paint and Coatings Association
1500 Rhode Island Avenue NW
Washington, D.C. 20005
Members/Purpose: Serves approximately 400 coatings manufacturers,
distributors, and raw materials suppliers.
Journals/Publications: Publishes a variety of brochures.
Training: Annual meeting; workshops and seminars.

APPENDIX

ADDITIONAL RESOURCES

American Ceramic Society Bulletin
P.O. Box 6136
Westerville, OH 43086

America's Teachers: An Introduction to Education
Addison-Wesley Publishing
1 Jacobs Way
Reading, MA 01867

"America's Teachers: Profile of a Profession"
National Center for Education Statistics
U.S. Department of Education
Office of Educational Research and Improvement
Washington, D.C. 20208

Braddock's Federal-State-Local Government Directory
Braddock Communications
909 North Washington Street
Alexandria, VA 22314

Canadian Journal of Chemical Engineering
Canadian Society for Chemical Engineering
130 Slater Street
Ottawa, Ontario
Canada K1P 6E2

Career Focus
Communications Publishing Group
106 West 11th Street
Kansas City, MO 64105

The Career Guide: Dun's Employment Opportunities Directory
Dun & Bradstreet
One Diamond Hill Road
Murray Hill, NJ 07974

Career Information Center
Macmillan Publishing Group
866 Third Avenue
New York, NY 10022

Career Opportunities in Cosmetic Science
Society of Cosmetic Chemists
120 Wall Street
New York, NY 10005

Career Woman
Equal Opportunity Publishing
150 Motor Parkway
Hauppage, NY 11788

Careers Encyclopedia
NTC/Contemporary Publishing Group
4255 West Touhy Avenue
Lincolnwood, IL 60646

Careers for Chemists
American Chemical Society
1155 16th Street NW
Washington, D.C. 20036

Careers for Environmental Types and Others Who Respect the Earth
NTC/Contemporary Publishing Group
4255 West Touhy Avenue
Lincolnwood, IL 60646

Careers in Education
NTC/Contemporary Publishing Group
4255 West Touhy Avenue
Lincolnwood, IL 60646

Careers in Teaching
Rosen Publishing
29 East 21st Street
New York, NY 10010

Chemical and Engineering News
American Chemical Society
1155 16th Street NW
Washington, D.C. 20036

Chemical Engineers
Chronicle Guidance Publications
66 Aurora Street
P.O. Box 1190
Moravia, NY 13118

Chemistry
Chronicle Guidance Publications
66 Aurora Street
P.O. Box 1190
Moravia, NY 13118

Chemistry and Your Career: Questions and Answers
American Chemical Society
1155 16th Street NW
Washington, D.C. 20036

Chem Tech
American Chemical Society
1155 16th Street NW
Washington, D.C. 20036

Chemunity News
American Chemical Society
1155 16th Street NW
Washington, D.C. 20036

Chicago Tribune
435 North Michigan Avenue
Chicago, IL 60611

The Chronicle of Higher Education
1255 23rd Street NW
Washington, D.C. 20037

Compendium of Environmental Training Courses and Programs
Canadian Council for Human Resources in the Environmental Industry
700 Fourth Avenue SW
Calgary, Alberta
Canada T2P 3J4

Current Jobs for Graduates
Plymouth Publishing, Inc.
P.O. Box 40550
Washington, D.C. 20016

Directory of Chemical Engineering Research in Canada
Canadian Society for Chemical Engineering
130 Slater Street
Ottawa, Ontario
Canada K1P 6E2

Directory of Directories
Gale Research, Inc.
P.O. Box 33477
Detroit, MI 48232

DISCOVER
American College Testing
Educational Services Division
P.O. Box 168
Iowa City, IA 52244

Discovering New Medicines: Careers in Pharmaceutical Research and Development
John Wiley and Sons
605 Third Avenue
New York, NY 10158

EEO Bimonthly
CASS Communications
1800 Sherman Avenue, Suite 300
Evanston, IL 60201

Federal Career Opportunities
Gordon Press Publishers
P.O. Box 459
Bowling Green Station
New York, NY 10004

Federal Jobs Digest
Breakthrough Publications
P.O. Box 594
Millwood, NY 10546

Government Job Finder
Planning Communications
7215 Oak Avenue
River Forest, IL 60305

The Handbook of Private Schools
Porter Sargent Publishers
11 Beacon Street, Suite 1400
Boston, MA 02108

Independent School
National Association of Independent Schools
1620 L Street NW
Washington, D.C. 20036

Index of Majors and Graduate Degrees
College Board Publications
P.O. Box 886
New York, NY 10101

Instructor Magazine
555 Broadway
New York, NY 10012

Internships
Peterson's Guides
Box 2123
Princeton, NJ 08543

Job Hotlines USA
Career Communications, Inc.
P.O. Box 169
Harleyville, PA 19438

Job Opportunities in Engineering and Technology
Peterson's Guides
Box 2123
Princeton, NJ 08543

Job Opportunities in the Environment
Peterson's Guides
Box 2123
Princeton, NJ 08543

The Job Source Series
2000 L Street NW
Washington, D.C. 20036

Journal of International Marketing
American Marketing Association
250 South Wacker Drive, Suite 200
Chicago, IL 60606

Journal of Marketing
American Marketing Association
250 South Wacker Drive, Suite 200
Chicago, IL 60606

Journal of the American Chemical Society
American Chemical Society
1155 16th Street NW
Washington, D.C. 20036

Journal of the Society of Cosmetic Chemists
Society of Cosmetic Chemists
120 Wall Street
New York, NY 10005

The Los Angeles Times
Times Mirror Square
Los Angeles, CA 90053

Marketing News
American Marketing Association
250 South Wacker Drive, Suite 200
Chicago, IL 60606

National Business Employment Weekly
Dow Jones & Company
P.O. Box 300
Princeton, NJ 08543

National Directory of Internships
National Society for Internships and Experiential Education
3509 Haworth Drive, Suite 207
Raleigh, NC 27609

National Teacher Exam
Educational Testing Service
P.O. Box 6051
Princeton, NJ 08541

The New York Times
229 West 43rd Street
New York, NY 10036

Non-Profits and Education Job Finder
Planning/Communications
7215 Oak Avenue
River Front, IL 60305

Occupational Outlook Handbook
Occupational Outlook Quarterly
U.S. Department of Labor
Bureau of Labor Statistics
Washington, D.C. 20212

Opportunities in Chemistry Careers
NTC/Contemporary Publishing Group
4255 West Touhy Avenue
Lincolnwood, IL 60646

Opportunities in Federal Government Careers
NTC/Contemporary Publishing Group
4255 West Touhy Avenue
Lincolnwood, IL 60646

Our Petroleum Challenge
Petroleum Resources Communication Foundation
633 6th Avenue SW
Calgary, Alberta
Canada T2P 2Y5

Patterson's American Education
Educational Directories, Inc.
P.O. Box 199
Mount Prospect, IL 60056

Planning for a Career in Chemistry
American Chemical Society
1155 16th Street NW
Washington, D.C. 20036

Planning for Graduate Work in Chemistry
American Chemical Society
1155 16th Street NW
Washington, D.C. 20036

Plastics Engineering
Society of Plastics Engineers
P.O. Box 403
Brookfield, CT 06804

Regional, State, and Local Organizations
Gale Research, Inc.
P.O. Box 33477
River Forest, IL 60305

Science
American Association for the Advancement of Science
1200 New York Avenue NW
Washington, D.C. 20005

Science Writers
Chronicle Guidance Publications
66 Aurora Street
P.O. Box 1190
Moravia, NY 13118

The Washington Post
1150 15th Street NW
Washington, D.C. 20071

Working for Your Uncle: The Complete Guide to Finding a Job in the Federal Government
Breakthrough Publications
310 North Highland Avenue
Ossining, NY 10562

INDEX